Apple Watch™

FOR

DUMMIES®

A Wiley Brand

Apple Watch™

FOR DUMMIES®
A Wiley Brand

by Marc Saltzman
Freelance journalist, author, speaker,
and radio and TV personality

FOR DUMMIES®
A Wiley Brand

Apple Watch™ For Dummies®

Published by: **John Wiley & Sons, Inc.,** 111 River Street, Hoboken, NJ 07030-5774, www.wiley.com

Copyright © 2015 by John Wiley & Sons, Inc., Hoboken, New Jersey

Published simultaneously in Canada

No part of this publication may be reproduced, stored in a retrieval system or transmitted in any form or by any means, electronic, mechanical, photocopying, recording, scanning or otherwise, except as permitted under Sections 107 or 108 of the 1976 United States Copyright Act, without the prior written permission of the Publisher. Requests to the Publisher for permission should be addressed to the Permissions Department, John Wiley & Sons, Inc., 111 River Street, Hoboken, NJ 07030, (201) 748-6011, fax (201) 748-6008, or online at http://www.wiley.com/go/permissions.

Trademarks: Wiley, For Dummies, the Dummies Man logo, Dummies.com, Making Everything Easier, and related trade dress are trademarks or registered trademarks of John Wiley & Sons, Inc. and may not be used without written permission. Apple Watch is a trademark of Apple, Inc. All other trademarks are the property of their respective owners. John Wiley & Sons, Inc. is not associated with any product or vendor mentioned in this book. *Apple Watch™ For Dummies®* is an independent publication and has not been authorized, sponsored, or otherwise approved by Apple, Inc.

LIMIT OF LIABILITY/DISCLAIMER OF WARRANTY: THE PUBLISHER AND THE AUTHOR MAKE NO REPRESENTATIONS OR WARRANTIES WITH RESPECT TO THE ACCURACY OR COMPLETENESS OF THE CONTENTS OF THIS WORK AND SPECIFICALLY DISCLAIM ALL WARRANTIES, INCLUDING WITHOUT LIMITATION WARRANTIES OF FITNESS FOR A PARTICULAR PURPOSE. NO WARRANTY MAY BE CREATED OR EXTENDED BY SALES OR PROMOTIONAL MATERIALS. THE ADVICE AND STRATEGIES CONTAINED HEREIN MAY NOT BE SUITABLE FOR EVERY SITUATION. THIS WORK IS SOLD WITH THE UNDERSTANDING THAT THE PUBLISHER IS NOT ENGAGED IN RENDERING LEGAL, ACCOUNTING, OR OTHER PROFESSIONAL SERVICES. IF PROFESSIONAL ASSISTANCE IS REQUIRED, THE SERVICES OF A COMPETENT PROFESSIONAL PERSON SHOULD BE SOUGHT. NEITHER THE PUBLISHER NOR THE AUTHOR SHALL BE LIABLE FOR DAMAGES ARISING HEREFROM. THE FACT THAT AN ORGANIZATION OR WEBSITE IS REFERRED TO IN THIS WORK AS A CITATION AND/OR A POTENTIAL SOURCE OF FURTHER INFORMATION DOES NOT MEAN THAT THE AUTHOR OR THE PUBLISHER ENDORSES THE INFORMATION THE ORGANIZATION OR WEBSITE MAY PROVIDE OR RECOMMENDATIONS IT MAY MAKE. FURTHER, READERS SHOULD BE AWARE THAT INTERNET WEBSITES LISTED IN THIS WORK MAY HAVE CHANGED OR DISAPPEARED BETWEEN WHEN THIS WORK WAS WRITTEN AND WHEN IT IS READ.

For general information on our other products and services, please contact our Customer Care Department within the U.S. at 877-762-2974, outside the U.S. at 317-572-3993, or fax 317-572-4002. For technical support, please visit www.wiley.com/techsupport.

Wiley publishes in a variety of print and electronic formats and by print-on-demand. Some material included with standard print versions of this book may not be included in ebooks or in print-on-demand. If this book refers to media such as a CD or DVD that is not included in the version you purchased, you may download this material at http://booksupport.wiley.com. For more information about Wiley products, visit www.wiley.com.

Library of Congress Control Number: 2014959619

ISBN 978-1-119-05205-0 (pbk); ISBN 978-1-119-05197-8 (ebk); ISBN 978-1-119-05196-1 (ebk)

Manufactured in the United States of America

10 9 8 7 6 5 4 3 2 1

Contents at a Glance

Table of Contents

Introduction

I'm excited to present you with *Apple Watch For Dummies* — your definitive guide to unlocking the power of your smartwatch.

In this book, you find out how to take full advantage of Apple Watch's many features — all in a language you can understand. You don't need a degree in electrical engineering to follow along with this book. Whether you're tech-shy or tech-savvy or perhaps somewhere in between, my goal is to teach you — in plain English — how to master your new gadget.

Apple Watch For Dummies covers all the things you can do with your sleek wrist-mounted companion, ranging from productivity and connectivity features to information, personalization, and navigation; health and fitness applications; entertainment options; and much more. And, of course, this book contains many visual examples of what you can do and what your watch should look like in certain situations.

About This Book

I wrote this book with one focus in mind: to cover all you need to know about Apple Watch in a language you can understand. I break down the geek-speak into street-speak.

After all, technology can be confusing, especially when it's a brand-new product like Apple Watch. Therefore, consider this book your definitive guide to unlocking Apple Watch's capabilities. Kind of like with our brains, it's estimated we use only about 10 percent of what our consumer electronics products can do — whether it's a computer, smartphone, tablet, TV, or camera — so it's my *modus operandi* to fill your head with the other 90 percent.

If you're more of an intermediate to advanced user, however, I also include a number of tips and tricks on how to get the most from your Apple Watch. But feel free to also experiment, which can be part of the fun. Apple Watch is a brand-new product, so it'll likely take some time to figure out all it can do.

Keep in mind that Apple will probably add new features to Apple Watch over "time" or when a new operating system update is available. But don't fret: This book covers not only just the basics but also advanced capabilities. And after you learn — and apply — a good number of the tasks discussed in this book, you should no doubt be comfortable with whatever new things the watch can do in the future.

On that note, Apple Watch is in its infancy, so you're probably as excited as I am to see how this platform will mature. Think about how far the iPhone is today compared with the first generation in 2007. Ditto for the latest iPad when contrasted with the original in 2010. The best, as they say, is yet to come. But this book covers everything you need to know right now.

Keep in mind that wearable technology like Apple Watch is a relatively new category. Don't be stressed out if it takes you some time to learn the new platform. You've probably used a computer for most of your life and a smartphone and/or tablet for the better part of a few years, but a smartwatch is an entirely different animal altogether.

You'll need to acclimate to the limited screen size, how to interact with the watch via your fingertips and voice, and what apps work best on your wrist (just as you'll discover some things are simply better on a phone). Because Apple Watch might have a possibly steeper learning curve than other technology, give yourself a while to master it. Just know I'm here to help in a language you can understand, which means you can put away your geek-to-English dictionary.

How to Use This Book

While this book is meant to be a handy and informative resource, I hope you find the tone conversational. And as with other *For Dummies* books, you can read *Apple Watch For Dummies* in any order you like. I'd suggest you start with the first chapter or two in order to learn the various parts of the watch and its user interface, but after that, feel free to jump from chapter to chapter if one topic interests you more than another. Perhaps start by thumbing through the specific topics in the Table of Contents and then go to a particular chapter that piques your curiosity.

For example, you might wonder about the fitness capabilities of Apple Watch — how it counts your steps and the number of stairs climbed, calculates distance traveled, determines your calories burned and heart rate, and so on — so you can turn to Chapter 8 right away. Or maybe you're anxious to master text messages, emails, and calls on your new device? That would be Chapter 5 — on keeping in touch with those who matter. On the other hand, Chapter 10 focuses on using Apple Watch for making mobile payments at retail by waving your wrist over a contactless terminal to complete a transaction.

You get the idea. Each chapter can stand on its own.

While chapters are divided by task, be aware that each one also has a few subtopics within it. For example, Chapter 6 is on using Apple Watch to stay informed, but the information is broken down into such topics as calendar appointments, maps, live sports scores, stock quotes, and weather information.

But if you're "old school" and would like a more linear read, go ahead and flip through it from beginning to end — just don't expect a plot twist near the end. (Spoiler alert: The butler did it.)

In some cases, I cross-reference subjects with topics from other chapters whenever relevant, but you can skip over them if you like or you can pursue them.

I also cover how to best use your voice instead of your fingertips — after all, I wrote the book *Siri For Dummies* (shameless plug alert!).

It goes without saying that you'll benefit most from this book if you have your Apple Watch with you, along with your nearby iPhone — which is required for many of the smartwatch's features to run — and if you ensure the battery is full on both devices so your lessons won't be interrupted. Oh, and it doesn't matter which Apple Watch you own — such as Apple Watch Sport (aluminum case), Apple Watch (stainless steel case), or Apple Watch Edition (18-karat gold case) — because this book is relevant to every model.

After trying many of the Apple Watch features I teach you in this book, expect to reach for your iPhone less and less. You'll likely hear this from seasoned Apple Watch users: Keep your iPhone tucked away in your pocket or purse but still access what you want by simply tapping or talking into your wrist. It's all about convenience.

The various tips and tricks throughout — as well as some interesting tidbits — will help you get the most from your Apple Watch. For example, you can use your Apple Watch to control music, audiobooks, and podcasts on your iPhone. Also, your watch knows the difference between a tap and a press. And did you know your watch can tap *you* with a slight vibration whenever a new message arrives for you to read? You learn how to do that — and much more — throughout this book.

But you don't need to wade through these extra Apple Watch factoids if you prefer to stick to the basics. Most of this extra content is labeled as Technical Stuff or Tip (see the "Icons Used in This Book" section). Then again, you might be more interested in these "sides" than the main course. (I'm sometimes like that when I visit my favorite restaurant.)

Also, be aware that this book has many figures, so you can see the steps — or the outcome of them — as you would on your own watch. This visual information should make it easier to follow along.

Foolish Assumptions

When writing this book, I made only two major assumptions:

- ✔ You own one of the Apple Watch products.
- ✔ You want to know how to get the most from it.

The watch won't come with an instruction manual, so consider *Apple Watch For Dummies* the closest thing to one — and a whole lot more too, if I may say so myself.

Oh, I actually made one more assumption: I assumed you also own an iPhone, which is required to gain the most from your wirelessly connected watch. For example, Apple Watch doesn't have a SIM card, so you won't be able to use it on its own to make calls, receive texts, check email, and so on.

Icons Used in This Book

The following icons are placed in the margins of the book's pages to point out information you may or may not want to read.

This icon offers suggestions to enhance your experience. Most are tied to the topic at hand, while others are more general in nature.

This icon reinforces the importance of information related to Apple Watch. You might consider bookmarking the page or jotting down the information elsewhere.

Apple Watch is a promising new wearable platform, but this icon alerts you to important considerations when using it, including health, safety, or security concerns.

This icon warns you about geeky descriptions or explanations you may want to pass on — but don't expect a lot of these throughout this easy-to-read guide.

Beyond This Book

We're almost ready to dive into this book so you can master your Apple Watch. It should be noted that a lot of excellent online information tied to Apple Watch exists, so the following are a few good websites to check out and potentially bookmark for future visits:

- **Dummies** (`www.dummies.com`): The official website for all the Dummies books, including sections on Apple Watch, iPhone, and Siri.

- **Apple Watch For Dummies** (`www.dummies.com/extras/applewatch`): This is where you can learn more about the Apple Watch collections, gain information about other smartwatches, and discover how Apple focused on time accuracy for Apple Watch.

- **Apple Watch For Dummies Cheat Sheet** (`www.dummies.com/cheatsheet/applewatch`): This site offers information discussed in this book but presented in different ways.

- **Apple Watch** (`www.apple.com/watch`): Apple's website for all things Apple Watch, including specifications, features, and an online store.

- **Wikipedia: Apple Watch** (`http://wikipedia.org/wiki/Apple_Watch`): A communally updated resource for Apple Watch, including links to other resources.

- **Gizmodo (Watch Section)** (`http://gizmodo.com/tag/watch`): A look at all watch-related information, photos, and reviews, including a ton of Apple Watch content.

- **9to5Mac** (`http://9to5mac.com`): A handy resource for all things Apple Watch, along with other Apple products.

- **Engadget** (`www.engadget.com`): Popular portal for consumer electronics, including coverage of Apple Watch news, reviews, and features.

- **The Loop** (`www.loopinsight.com`): Coverage of gadgets, apps, and other techy trends but with a strong focus on Apple products.

- **C|Net's Apple Watch page** (`www.cnet.com/products/apple-watch`): Apple Watch news, reviews, and features tied to Apple's first wearable.

Where to Go From Here

If you've never used an Apple Watch — perhaps you bought this book in anticipation of purchasing one or receiving it as a gift — it might be best to power up the watch, turn it on, and follow the prompts to set it all up. Chapter 2 goes into this if you prefer to wait or feel free to dive in with the watch before you fully crack the spine of this book. Your call based on your comfort level.

Regardless of which model you own — or plan on buying or receiving — you don't need to know anything to begin reading *Apple Watch For Dummies*. All you need is your willingness to learn this exciting new wearable gadget, which should help add convenience, speed, and style to your everyday tasks.

Ready to start? Turn the page. . . .

Part I
Getting to Know Apple Watch

For more on the Apple Watch collections and how Apple Watch compares with similar smartwatches, visit www.dummies.com/extras/applewatch.

In this part . . .

✔ Learn how to set up your Apple Watch and discover its many features, including the Digital Crown button and the Side button, and what aspects of Apple Watch make it unique from your iPhone.

✔ Pair your Apple Watch with your iPhone and then learn about setting up a PIN, monitoring battery usage, and protecting your valuable investment.

✔ Explore the many ways you can interact with your Apple Watch, including tapping, pressing, and swiping as well as using Siri to help you complete tasks with your Apple Watch.

1

Watch This: Introducing Apple Watch

....

In This Chapter

▶ Understanding the different Apple Watch models

▶ Learning about the many features of Apple Watch

▶ Navigating the Home screen

▶ Exploring different parts of Apple Watch

▶ Understanding wireless capabilities and sensors

....

*S*o, are you excited or what?

You're one of the first in the world to own an Apple Watch. Or perhaps you purchased this book in anticipation of picking one up or receiving it as a gift. Either way, thank you for reading *Apple Watch For Dummies*. This easy-to-read book has one goal in mind: to teach you everything you need to know about Apple Watch. With simple step-by-step instructions, clear images, and accessible tips and tricks, this book will help you gain the most from your new wearable gadget.

In this chapter, I walk you through the basics of Apple Watch to help you discover what this teeny wrist-mounted computer is capable of. Find out about the different parts of the watch — on the outside and inside — as well as the layout of the Home screen. From ways to interface with content on the watch to the hidden wireless technologies to integrated sensors that track your moves, you should soon see a clear picture of the 21st-century magic you're wearing on your wrist.

Exploring the Different Apple Watch Collections

Apple Watch comes in two different sizes: 38 millimeters (about 1.5 inches) and 42 millimeters (roughly 1.65 inches). This measurement is from the top of the Apple Watch screen to the bottom and not diagonally — like how most screens from consumer electronics are measured (such as smartphones, tablets, laptops, and TVs).

Although most people likely already bought a watch before buying this book, I want to briefly mention the three Apple Watch collections — shown in Figure 1-1 — and a few accessories you can purchase to customize your watch. For a more extensive discussion about the Apple Watch collections — for when you need to convince a friend or coworker that he or she needs an Apple Watch — see www.dummies.com/extras/applewatch.

Figure 1-1: The Apple Watch Sport, Apple Watch Edition, and Apple Watch versions, respectively.

The three Apple Watch collections are:

- **Apple Sport Watch:** This is for those who want something lightweight yet durable. It's made from anodized aluminum and with sweat-resistant fluoroelastomer (synthesized rubber) in five sporty colors: white, black, blue, green, and pink.

- **Apple Watch Edition:** This is for those who appreciate — and can afford — luxury. The retina display is protected by polished sapphire crystal and accessory choices include a number of unique straps and bands with 18-karat gold clasps, buckles, or pins.

- **Apple Watch:** This is a little more expensive because it comes in highly polished stainless steel or matted black stainless steel and offers a variety of band choices: leather, fluoroelastomer, Milanese loop, and link bracelet.

Figuring Out What Apple Watch Can Do

Some may question why they *need* a smartwatch. Perhaps you traded your watch for a smartphone years ago and now wonder why you'd go back to the wrist? One word: convenience. Not having to carrying anything is pretty darn handy, which you soon find out when using your Apple Watch. Simply glance at your wrist to glean information — wherever and whenever you need it — not to mention your watch can *tap* you with a slight tactile vibration to let you know about something, such as a calendar appointment or a loved one giving you a virtual "poke." Buying something at a vending machine or a retail store by simply waving your wrist over a sensor is all kinds of awesome. Or having an airline attendant scan a barcode on your watch's screen to let you board a plane? What a time-saver.

You can thus keep your iPhone tucked away, preserving its battery for when you really need to access something with it.

Perhaps because you wear it on your wrist and will likely glance at it multiple times throughout the day, Apple Watch will become an extension of yourself. When you strap this baby onto your wrist, you're not going to want to take it off. Now, that's personal.

As you discover in this book, Apple Watch has many, many features. Some of its main categories include time, communication, information, navigation, fitness, entertainment, and finance (mobile payments).

The following sections highlight Apple Watch's main components.

Watch faces

Instead of a regular watch that simply shows one face, you can choose what to see on your Apple Watch. The watch has many styles to choose from right out of the box and many downloadable apps to also customize the look of the face. You can also change the color of the watch face to match your outfit. Chapter 4 walks you through it all.

Timers and alarms

Apple Watch also includes various stopwatches, timers, and alarms. Whether you use your fingertips or your voice, your Apple Watch can let you know when it's been 30 minutes so you can pull something from the oven. Or time your friend doing laps in a pool — from the comfort of your lounge chair. Apple Watch also lets you set an alarm to wake you up in the morning. The Timer app can be used as a game clock, for example, to tell you and your opponent when your time is up in a round of Scrabble. Check out Chapter 4 for all the details.

Caller ID

See who's calling by glancing at your wrist. Apple Watch displays the caller's name (Caller ID) or perhaps just a phone number (which often happens if that person isn't in your iPhone's Contacts). You can also use the Apple Watch microphone to record and send sound clips to friends with a new walkie-talkie–like app. Heed the call and go to Chapter 5 for details.

Text messages

You can read and reply to text messages with Apple Watch, as shown in Figure 1-2. Hold your wrist up to read the message or lower your arm to dismiss it. Chapter 5 walks you through all the text messaging functions for Apple Watch.

Figure 1-2: Read and reply to messages on your Apple Watch.

Email

When an email comes in, you can read it on your wrist (scroll up and down the screen with your fingertip to see all the text), flag it as something to reply to later, mark it as read (or unread), or move it to the Trash. As with text messages and phone calls, you can transfer email from Apple Watch to your iPhone to pick up where you left off. I cover all this in Chapter 5.

Wrist-to-wrist communication

Your smartwatch lets you communicate directly with someone else's wrist via a component called *Digital Touch*. For a sketch, use your fingertip to draw something, such as the heart shown in Figure 1-3, and the person who receives it will see

Figure 1-3: Sketch something on your Apple Watch and then send it off to someone else's Apple Watch.

it animate — just as you drew it. A feature called a *tap* lets someone know you're thinking about him or her. As described in Chapter 5, you can even send your heartbeat to someone by pressing two fingers on the screen.

Friends ring

Press the Side button on Apple Watch to bring up your Friends ring. You see initials along the edges of the ring, but a person's first name is in the top-left corner when you land on that person's details. In the center, you should see thumbnail photos of that person or a silhouette if you don't have a photo of him or her in your iPhone's Contacts app. Twist the Digital Crown button to select someone and then press in. Now you can choose a person to send a message, to call, or to engage with by using one of the Digital Touch features. Flip to Chapter 3 to learn more about the Digital Crown button and Chapter 5 for more on your Friends ring.

Glances

Naturally, a wearable watch is a convenient way to stay on top of important information. As such, Apple Watch has a cool feature called *Glances* that — as the name suggests — lets app developers create one glanceable summary of information you can see when you swipe up from the bottom of your watch, as shown in Figure 1-4. Chapter 6 tells you how to access Glances, customize what you see, and scroll through relevant information.

Figure 1-4: Glances allow you to see — what else? — quick glances about specific information related to topics you choose.

Calendars

Apple Watch also has a Calendar app (with reminders) so you can stay on top of events throughout your day (or coming in the near future). Also, when you receive a calendar invitation, you can immediately accept or decline it on your wrist and even email preset responses to the organizer. Put Chapter 6 on your calendar for more information.

Maps

Your wrist is an ideal place to glance at a map. Get turn-by-turn directions from your current location — and you don't have to worry about having to stare at your wrist for visual cues (or fall down a manhole in the process) because Apple Watch gives you a tap on the wrist to let you know when it's time to turn left or right. Navigate to Chapter 6 for more.

Siri

Just as you can talk into your phone, Apple Watch also has a microphone, which means you can have access to your personal assistant known as Siri. Flip to Chapter 7 to find out more about what Siri can do for you. As the author of *Siri For Dummies*, I share some of my favorite Siri tips and tricks you can master with ease.

Fitness

One of the coolest applications for Apple Watch? Fitness. Chapter 8 looks at using the watch to measure your activity — steps, stairs, distance, time, calories burned, and heart rate information — and to display it in a meaningful way on your watch and smartphone. I cover the Activity app, shown in Figure 1-5, and its three rings, which show you relevant information on your daily

Figure 1-5: The Activity app shows three rings that summarizes your daily progress — so far.

activity (or lack thereof!). On the other hand, the Workout app (as shown in Figure 1-6) offers some workout routine options — including walking, jogging, running, and cycling — and shows real-time stats on your cardio session.

Figure 1-6: The Workout app offers you some different exercise routines.

iTunes connectivity

Chapter 9 teaches you how to use Apple Watch like a wireless remote. Control your music on your phone — from the convenience of your wrist — as well as listen to synced playlists on your watch *without* needing your iPhone (but with Bluetooth headphones). Along with talking about music (including accessing iTunes Radio), I highlight how to manage podcasts, audiobooks, radio plays, and other audio. Chapter 9 also covers how to control Apple TV on your Apple Watch.

Apple Pay

Swiping your wrist at retail stores or at a vending machine is super cool — and Chapter 10 covers all the ways you can use your Apple Watch in this regard. Your watch lets you buy products and services via Apple Pay — and you don't even need your iPhone with you.

Other apps

Apple Watch is quite a versatile gadget, which means other apps can help enhance its convenience. Chapter 11 looks at a number of optional third-party apps you can download to further personalize the most personal gadget in the world.

Other functions

Chapter 12 takes a closer look at some of the extra fun things you can do with Apple Watch. I cover using your wrist to remotely snap a photo on your iPhone as well as look at photos on your wrist, including how to zoom into a photo (because maybe you're bored in line at the supermarket and want to see some smiling faces or furry pets). I also discuss Apple Watch as a gaming platform and what's available.

Bonus tips

Chapter 13 reveals the top ten things you should try with Apple Watch — and, of course, how to pull them off with grace. I share the absolute coolest things this smartwatch can do and how to best demonstrate it to your friends to the point they'll be boiling with envy.

Apple says you could squeeze up to 72 hours of battery life on Apple Watch, but be aware this varies greatly on how often you use the watch, the settings you choose (see Chapter 2), what apps you use, outside temperature, and other factors. Apple says most people will find it lasts up to 18 hours — hence, the "all day" estimate — based on the company's testing in March 2015. The test involved 90 time checks, 90 Notifications, 45 minutes of app use, and a 30-minute workout with music playback from Apple Watch via Bluetooth.

Determining What You Need for Your Apple Watch

Apple Watch doesn't do much on its own. Think of it as a companion device to an iPhone. Oh, sure, it can do a few things by itself — such as show you the time, count your steps, make payments, and play music — but a wirelessly tethered iPhone is required for the overwhelming majority of features.

To use Apple Watch, you need an iPhone 5 or newer, such as an iPhone 5, iPhone 5c, iPhone 5s, iPhone 6, or iPhone 6 Plus (or whatever comes out next, such as iPhone 7). You also need to download and install the iOS 8.2 (or later) operating system update from Apple — whether you do it on your iPhone or on iTunes (on a PC or Mac) — and then connect the iPhone to your computer with a USB cable. After you download iOS 8.2, an Apple Watch app — a white watch against a black background — appears on your iPhone's Home screen, as shown in Figure 1-7.

Figure 1-7: When you upgrade your iPhone's operating system to iOS 8.2 or later, the Apple Watch app (shown at top right) appears on your iPhone's Home screen.

You don't need a computer to use Apple Watch nor do you need an iPad or iPod touch or anything else. You just need a compatible iPhone.

Getting to Know the Apple Watch Home Screen

As shown in Figure 1-8, the main Home screen of the Apple Watch is populated by a number of small bubble-like icons. It's quite neat actually, not to mention functional. Simply tap an icon with your fingertip to open an app or slide around the Home screen to see other icons pop up and grow larger — with the app you want centered on the screen for easy access.

If you're an iPhone user, the icons should be familiar to you; therefore, you know what built-in and third-party apps launch when you tap a specific icon. Table 1-1 shows some of the built-in apps. See Chapter 3 for more on the native Apple Watch apps.

Figure 1-8: Press and move your finger around to see all the apps on your Home screen (or twist the Digital Crown button to zoom in and out).

As noted in Chapter 11, you don't download Apple Watch apps on the watch itself. Instead, you use an iPhone or Mac/PC to download apps for Apple Watch via the Apple Watch Store.

And, of course, third-party apps have their familiar icons, such as a big P for Pinterest, a "swoosh" for Nike, a green leaf for the Mint app, and so on. You can bet many thousands of developers will have their apps working on Apple Watch right out of the gate — but be patient in case some of your favorites aren't ready just yet. And some just might not make sense on a watch, such as an epic fantasy role-playing game that works better with a larger screen.

Table 1-1	Built-In Apple Watch Apps
App	*Icon*
Clock	
Phone	
Messages	
Email	
Calendar	
Maps	
Music	
Weather	

App	*Icon*
Photos	
Remote Camera	
Settings	
Passbook	
Stopwatch	
Alarm	
Activity	
Workout	

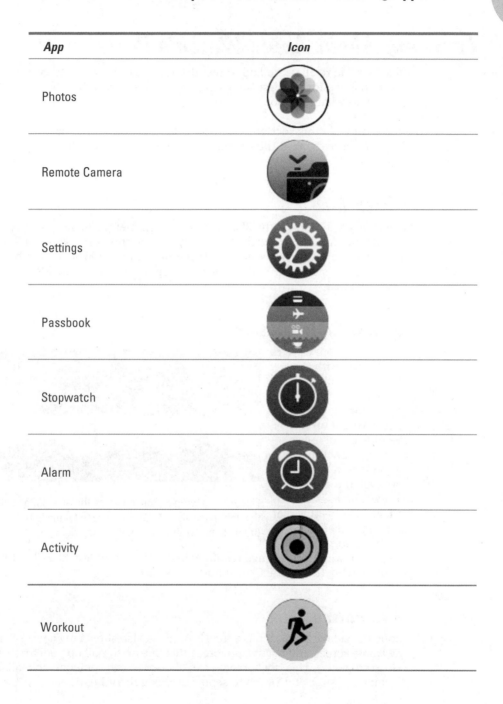

Learning About Apple Watch's Parts

Okay, so you're all geared up to test drive all that Apple Watch can do, but if you're using it for the first time, you may not even know all the parts of the watch and what they do.

Fair enough. In this section, you discover the basics of the hardware itself. We start with a look at the various parts of the watch on the outside and what they do.

Watch face

Whether you opted for the 38 mm or 42 mm model (referring to its vertical height), the Apple Watch face is entirely digital; therefore, you won't find any buttons of any kind. Use your fingertip to move around the icon bubbles and tap an app to launch it. You can also tap, press, and swipe inside an app to perform a task.

Digital Crown button

Seasoned watch owners are familiar with the small rotary dial on a watch's right side (usually), which is used to either wind it up (for the old-school ones anyway) or set the time. Apple Watch has one too. Called the *Digital Crown button* — shown in Figure 1-9 — this dial can be pressed, tapped, or turned forward or backward, with each change resulting in a different action. See Chapter 3 for more on what the Digital Crown button can do.

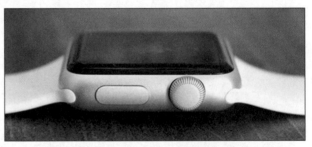

Figure 1-9: If worn on the left wrist, the Side button will be on the right-hand side of the watch case (at the left). The Digital Crown button is the ridged dial on the right.

Side button

Along the side of the watch is a long button, as also shown in Figure 1-9. From the Home screen and in any app, press this button to pull up your Friends ring (close contacts). This is where you can choose to call someone or send a text or email or use Digital Touch to send a tap, sketch, or heartbeat.

Back sensors/charger

On the back of Apple Watch, as shown in Figure 1-10, are four sensors to monitor your heart rate (measured in beats per minute). A larger circle surrounding the four smaller heart rate sensors is used to charge up the Apple Watch battery. See Chapter 2 for more on the sensors and the charger.

Watch band

Every wristwatch has a band to keep the screen snug on your wrist. You chose a specific band when you bought Apple Watch — whether a leather strap, a link bracelet, a classic buckle, or a silicone band — but you can change bands later if you desire.

You don't need to press hard on these buttons or on the watch face. You want to minimize the wear and tear of your new (and pricey!) gadget. Just a simple press on the buttons and watch face will do. Also, try to avoid touching the screen and buttons with wet or damp hands. Electronics and water don't exactly go well together. See Chapter 3 for more on these buttons and using your fingers with your Apple Watch.

Figure 1-10: Check out these cool sensors on the back of Apple Watch. Among other things, they can calculate your heart rate.

Location, location, location

Despite nearly 200 countries on Earth, only nine of them received Apple Watch when it debuted on April 24, 2015: Australia, Canada, China, France, Germany, Hong Kong, Japan, the United Kingdom, and the United States. If you're reading this, perhaps you're one of the lucky ones? Apple hasn't disclosed why these markets were chosen, but just be happy if you're in one of them.

Using Apple Watch's Touchscreen

Just like you can interface with a smartphone, tablet, and laptop in different ways — based on the task at hand — Apple Watch gives you three ways to use the small screen on your wrist:

- ✔ **Tap:** Tapping with one finger on Apple Watch performs the same function as you'd expect on a smartphone: It selects whatever you're tapping, such as an icon to launch an app, a song to play a track, a link to a website, a photo to enlarge, or virtual buttons, such as on a calculator. On the Home screen, you tap and slide your finger around to move the icon bubbles. A tap is like a left-mouse click on a computer.

- ✔ **Press:** Apple Watch knows the difference between a quick tap and a longer press — usually when you need to open up some additional menus. Think of it as a kind of right-mouse click. For example, tapping a song plays the track, but pressing and holding it opens up a set of options: Shuffle, Repeat, Source, and AirPlay. The technology that senses the difference between a tap and a press is called *Force Touch*.

- ✔ **Swipe:** Glances are a quick look at content that's relevant to you — be it the score of your favorite team's current or last game, weather information, stock quotes, time to your destination (via Apple Maps), and so on. It's just one screen (that is, no scrolling), but swiping to the right on your watch face gives you this bite-sized information — when and where you need it.

Some features are activated with two fingers pressed on the screen. In Chapter 5, you can find out how to record and send your heart rate or heartbeat to a loved one's Apple Watch.

Understanding Apple Watch's Wireless Functions and Internal Sensors

Oh, Apple Watch, you cleverly hide so much of your magic under your skin.

While Apple isn't revealing much about the "brains" of Apple Watch — a system-on-a-chip called the *S1* — a more interesting dissection is perhaps all the other goodies that make Apple Watch a fully functional wearable.

Apple Watch indeed houses a good number of wireless radios beneath its surface, including Bluetooth, Wi-Fi, GPS, NFC, and more. To better understand what they do, consider the following sections.

Bluetooth 4.0

Bluetooth makes a local wireless connection between two or more devices. Just as your wireless headset is paired with your smartphone so you can make hands-free calls, Apple Watch wirelessly communicates with a nearby iPhone. This lets you see texts on your watch, receive phone calls, control your music on your phone, and more. Bluetooth 4.0 works with devices up to 200 feet away (compared to just 30 feet with earlier versions).

Wi-Fi 802.11b/g

Apple Watch also features Wi-Fi, which gives it online connectivity — even when no iPhone is in sight. As long as you're on a wireless network, such as your home's Internet connection or a coffee shop's hotspot, you can access such information as email, live sports scores, mapping information, and so on. A feature called *Continuity* — introduced in iOS 8 — means you can also receive messages and take calls on multiple iOS devices (such as answering a call on your iPad) as long as you're in range of your Wi-Fi network — and Apple Watch can do this too. See Chapter 5 for how to take advantage of Bluetooth and Wi-Fi connectivity.

NFC (near field communication)

NFC is a short-range radio technology (like Bluetooth) that has a number of applications but is most commonly associated with mobile payments. Similar to waving or tapping your iPhone 6 or iPhone 6 Plus on a contactless terminal at retail locations (or a compatible vending machine) to make a secure purchase, Apple Watch also uses NFC to make a *digital handshake* with the terminal to complete the transaction. Yep, it's all in the wrist. This is part of Apple Pay, Apple's mobile payment solution for secure cash- and card-less payments. Check out Chapter 10 for more on Apple Pay.

GPS (on the iPhone)

While Apple Watch doesn't have GPS, it works with the iPhone's GPS chip to identify its location on Earth — down to a few meters of accuracy. Therefore, when coupled with mapping applications, GPS can help you see your location on a map, get directions from point A to point B, look for local businesses of interest, and more. GPS can also help with tracking fitness data when measuring steps won't help (such as in cycling). Along with the accelerometer (discussed next), built-in heart rate sensor, and Wi-Fi, Apple Watch's GPS can help measure distance traveled. Jog on over to Chapter 8 to learn more about the Activity and Workout apps.

Accelerometer

As with other smartwatches and activity bands on the market, Apple Watch has an accelerometer that measures movement — whether you're lifting the watch to your face to turn on the screen, lowering your wrist to not accept a call, or calculating fitness activities, including your steps taken (like a 21st-century pedometer), total distance traveled, time spent exercising, and estimated calories burned.

Heart rate sensor

A custom heart rate sensor included with Apple Watch helps gauge your intensity during exercise and improves overall calorie tracking. It listens to your heart's beats per minute (BPM) and shows you data on the screen — if and when you call for it. Behind the watch are four sensors that measure your pulse through your skin. Going beyond fitness are the fun applications too, such as sharing your heartbeat with someone — felt on his or her Apple Watch — to show you're thinking about that person. See Chapter 5 for how to share this information to your heart's content.

Tapping With Apple Watch's Haptic Feedback

You can tap Apple Watch's screen, but guess what? It can tap you too.

As with video game controllers that vibrate (when your soldier gets shot) or some smartphones and tablets (that slight *buzz* when you tap a letter on the virtual keyboard), Apple Watch employs *haptic technology* to apply light force to your skin about relevant information.

Apple calls it *Taptic Engine*, a linear actuator inside the watch that produces discreet haptic feedback.

Consider this slight vibration a third sense (touch), along with sight and sound, to give you information. The physical sensation of a tap tells you something, such as an important meeting is about to start (without even having to look down at your wrist). It can be a silent alarm clock to wake you up in the morning instead of bothering your significant other. Or feeling your loved one's heartbeat even though he or she may be miles way.

What's more, Apple Watch can tap different patterns based on who's reaching out to you (such as two taps for your spouse and three taps for your boss) or perhaps the haptic pattern tells you what the information is (one tap for the time on the hour, four taps for a calendar appointment, and so on).

Neat, huh?

In the near future, Apple Watch's haptic feedback may let you know about important health information — perhaps when working in conjunction with sensors. Imagine if someone living with diabetes could feel a haptic tap on the skin to tell him or her it's time to take insulin based on the body's blood sugar levels.

2

Time Out: Setting Up Your Apple Watch

- -

In This Chapter

▶ Setting up the watch for first-time use

▶ Choosing a PIN

▶ Charging up Apple Watch

▶ Taking care of your smartwatch

▶ Using Apple Watch responsibly

▶ Taking advantage of accessibility features

- -

*W*ell, you did it. You're now the proud owner of an Apple Watch.

Or perhaps you received one as a gift and you're more intimidated than proud?

Regardless, I'm thrilled you picked up (or downloaded) this book to help you get the most from your wearable companion. You're gonna love your new gadget.

This chapter helps you set up Apple Watch for the first time as well as covers how to charge it up, take care of it, and get to know some of the basics.

Setting Up Apple Watch

If you're a fan of those unboxing videos on YouTube, you've watched a few gadget geeks excitedly open a box for the first time and expose all the goodies inside, but if you don't have the time or desire for that drama, let me tell you what you can expect if you haven't received your Apple Watch just yet or what you should find in your box if you have.

In your Apple Watch box, you should find:

- Apple Watch
- Extra Sport Band (Apple Watch Sport model only)
- Magnetic dock charger cable (USB cable)
- Five-watt power adaptor (white plug for the wall)
- Small booklet with setup and maintenance tips
- Plastic travel box with wrist strap insert (Apple Watch)
- Leather-lined jewelry box that doubles as a charger (Apple Watch Edition only)

The Apple Watch and Apple Watch Edition boxes are mostly square, compared to a longer and more rectangular Apple Watch Sport box. Be sure to keep the box and all the things inside just in case you need to return or exchange the watch.

Like many consumer electronics you buy today, the watch might be already charged up when you first get it, but it's always a good idea to plug it into a computer or the wall to give it a full boost before using it for the first time. This way, you won't run out of juice while playing around with the watch's settings, learning the mechanics, and so on.

Pairing Apple Watch with the iPhone

After you ensure your smartwatch is charged up, the next step is to tap the Apple Watch app on your iPhone. The app appears on your iPhone's Home screen after you've updated to the 8.2 operating system (and you can't remove it!). If you don't see the app on your phone's Home screen, swipe left or right to look for it. Remember, you need an iPhone 5 or newer and the 8.2 iOS operating system installed to use Apple Watch. To double-check what you have, tap Settings⇨General⇨About and look where it says Version. Your phone also notifies you about an available update.

Once you open the app, simply tap the Start Pairing tab near the bottom of the screen and then follow the prompts, which ask you to hold Apple Watch up to the iPhone's camera and then you can align the watch's face within the viewfinder in the center of the screen. This should do the trick.

See Figures 2-1 and 2-2 for a look at setting up Apple Watch for the first time.

Figure 2-1: The Apple Watch app first asks you to pair your Apple Watch.

Figure 2-2: Match up the Apple Watch inside the outline on your iPhone screen.

If that doesn't work, tap the Pair Apple Watch Manually option, in orange, at the bottom of the app. You're prompted to tap the "i" ("information") app on your Apple Watch to view its name and then tap the corresponding name listed in the app. If it's not listed, be sure your wireless connection is enabled; therefore, swipe up from the bottom of the screen and tap the icons for Bluetooth and Wi-Fi so they're highlighted and not grayed out.

Once the pairing is successful, you can adjust some of the watch's settings from within the app by tapping My Watch at the bottom left of the screen. You can also select Explore (in the bottom center of the app) to watch videos of Apple Watch or select App Store (bottom right of the app screen) to download and install third-party apps to your device.

Keep in mind that you don't need to turn Apple Watch on or off. Simply raise your wrist and the screen turns on — thanks to its internal accelerometer (motion sensor) — and lower your arm to turn it off. It's that easy.

Choosing a PIN for Apple Watch

While not mandatory — unless you use Apple Pay to buy goods or services through your smartwatch; see Chapter 10 for more on Apple Pay — those who use Apple Watch can set up a personal identification number (PIN) in case the watch is lost or stolen. (Some people call it a *passcode* instead of a PIN, but it's the same thing.)

It might not provide much comfort for those who break the bank for the top-of-the-line 18-karat gold Apple Watch Edition (!), but it still means no one can access your information or shop via Apple Pay.

Just like with an iPhone, iPad, or iPod touch, if the Apple Watch's PIN option is activated, you have to enter the four-digit numeric code every time you put the watch back on. Apple Pay requires skin contact and the PIN. See Figure 2-3 for setting up a PIN on Apple Watch.

Wait, how does Apple Watch "know" if someone is taking the watch off or putting it on? It's because of the smartwatch's internal sensors that touch your skin. I cover this more in Chapter 10, where I also go over what to do if you lose your Apple Watch. (Hint: As with a lost iPhone, you can go to www.icloud.com, log in with your details, and remove your credit and debit cards to prevent the watch from falling into the wrong hands.)

Bottom line: You may want to set up a passcode on your Apple Watch — even if you don't activate Apple Pay.

And, of course, you should also have a PIN set up on your iPhone. Remember, Apple Watch doesn't store much information, so protecting the data on your phone is even more important.

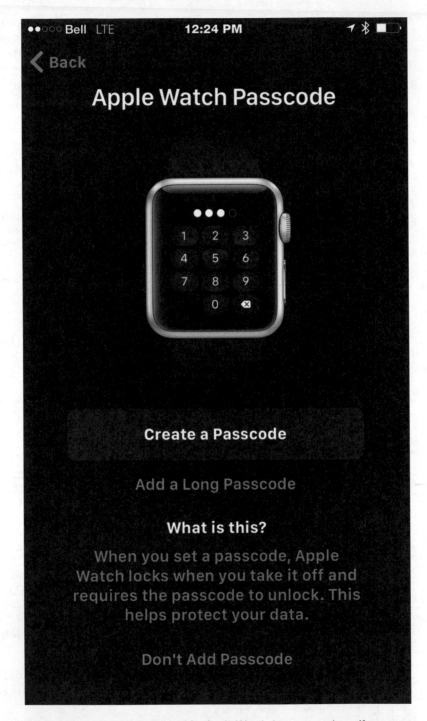

Figure 2-3: A passcode is optional for Apple Watch, but you need one if you want to use Apple Pay.

Monitoring the Apple Watch battery

One of the biggest challenges of such small technology that's always on? Battery life.

Thus, Apple gave its engineers a challenge to squeeze all-day performance out of Apple Watch. And they succeeded.

Okay, so *all-day performance* is a little vague, but Apple says it amounts to about 18 hours — based on Apple's testing on a 38 mm "preproduction Apple Watch and software paired with an iPhone using preproduction software," conducted in March 2015.

Apple Watch includes a magnetic charging cable: One end snaps onto the back of the smartwatch and is secured by a magnetic connection — not unlike Apple's MagSafe charger for MacBook laptops — and the other end of the cable can plug into a computer's powered USB port (Mac or PC) or into a traditional electrical socket (with supplied adaptor on the end).

As you might've noticed — in this text or after looking in the box Apple Watch came in — the USB cable doesn't plug into Apple Watch anywhere. Unlike some other smartwatches, you have no port to uncover. Instead, the circular puck magnetically affixes to the underside of the watch, where the heart rate sensors are, and powers up the watch through induction technology.

The magnetic charger makes it easy to juice up the Apple Watch because you don't have to open any ports on the watch to plug in a cable. Just attach it to the back of your Apple Watch, it snaps into place, and you're good to go.

See Figure 2-4 for a look at the unique Apple Watch charger.

Broken down, the 18-hour battery life includes the following:

- ✔ Ninety (90) time checks (four seconds long apiece)
- ✔ Receiving 90 Notifications
- ✔ Forty-five (45) minutes of app use
- ✔ A 30-minute workout with music playback via the iPhone and with heart rate monitoring enabled

A 42 mm Apple Watch typically experiences longer battery life, says Apple. The company also cautions that "battery life varies by use, configuration, and many other factors; actual results will vary."

If you're curious about specific tasks, Apple breaks down battery performance even further (based on a preproduction 38 mm watch):

- ✔ **Talk time test:** Up to three hours. Apple Watch was paired with an iPhone during the call.

- ✔ **Audio playback test:** Up to 6.5 hours (when paired via Bluetooth with an iPhone).

- ✔ **Workout test:** Up to 6.5 hours. Apple Watch was paired with an iPhone and had a workout session active and the heart rate sensor turned on.

- ✔ **Watch test:** Up to 48 hours. This test was composed of five time checks per hour (each for four seconds).

- ✔ **Power Reserve:** Up to 72 hours. Apple says its watch automatically switches to Power Reserve mode — when Apple Watch has only 10 percent battery remaining — so you can see the time up to 72 hours.

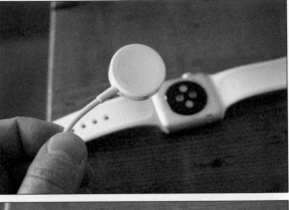

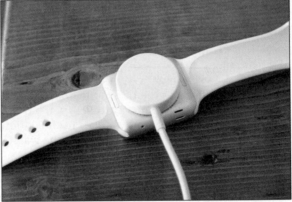

Figure 2-4: Apple Watch has no USB ports — just connect this magnetic puck to the back of the watch and plug the other end into a computer.

As Apple suggests, you likely want to charge up the watch at the end of each day to get it ready for the following one. If you only use the watch to tell time, you can get two or three days out of the watch without having to charge it up (but you can't do anything other than see the time in Power Reserve mode). Should you want it, more information about battery life is available at `apple.com/watch/battery.html`.

Battery-related accessories for Apple Watch

If you're on the go and don't want to worry about plugging the watch in somewhere to juice up, a number of power-centric products can help.

One called the Nomad Pod (about $60) — shown on the left — is a portable battery charger for the Apple Watch, featuring an 1,800-milliamp (mAh) battery. Nomad says this solution can provide up to four full charges for Apple Watch — before the Pod needs charging up.

Available in silver or space gray aluminum or black polycarbonate plastic, the Pod powers up the watch through magnetic induction and a USB port is used to power up the Pod for when you need it.

Nomad is also making a desktop charger for Apple Watch, aptly called Stand ($60). The aluminum-based Stand — shown on the right — holds the magnetic watch charger in a cradle, which could be fed through to the back of the stand to reduce clutter.

Understanding the Home Screen

Although you can customize what app you see first, by default, the clock is what appears when you look at the watch. If you press the Digital Crown button, however, you can access your Home screen to see all the apps installed on the watch.

Apple Watch's Home screen, as shown in Figure 2-5, is similar to other iOS devices — namely, iPhone, iPad, and iPod touch — as you see a bunch of icons that launch an app when you tap one.

The Home screen apps include Apple's own first-party applications — such as a speech bubble for messaging or a cloud with a sun peeking behind it for weather — as well as any third-party apps you choose to install and transfer to the watch from your iPhone, which might include a social media feed, such as Twitter; news information provided by CNN; or a game, such as Trivia Crack. You can see many of the native apps for Apple Watch in Table 1-1 in Chapter 1.

Figure 2-5: While they're bubbles instead of square icons (on iPhone and iPad), your Home screen apps should still look familiar to you.

But instead of neatly arranged rows and columns of app icons on an iPhone or iPad, apps on an Apple Watch are arranged like bubbles in different sizes that move around when you press and slide your finger around the Home screen. The apps grow larger when the icons become closer to the center of the Apple Watch screen, which makes them easier to tap and launch.

If you twist the Digital Crown button while on the Home screen, you can zoom in and out of all the apps you have installed on the watch. Pro tip: If you zoom enough on one app, Apple Watch launches it for you! Also, while you're in the Clock app, you can simply press the Digital Crown button to return to the Home screen.

You choose which apps are installed on Apple Watch via the Apple Watch app on your iPhone (preinstalled with iOS 8.2 and newer). An Apple Watch App Store is also built into the Apple Watch app for iPhone to allow you to download and manage your apps right from within the app. See Chapter 11 for installing third-party apps.

See Figure 2-6 for a look at the Apple Watch app on iPhone.

If you hold the Digital Crown button down for more than a second, it launches Siri, your personal voice-activated assistant (or simply say "Hey, Siri" into your watch). Only a quick tap on the Digital Crown button is necessary to open your Home screen. See Chapter 7 for more on using Siri on your Apple Watch.

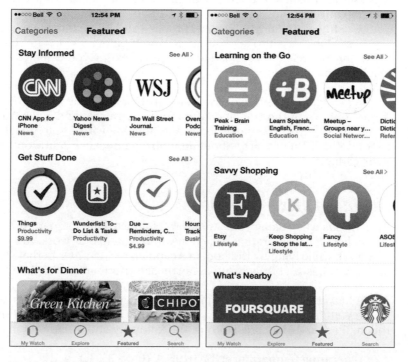

Figure 2-6: Tap the Featured tab inside the Apple Watch app on your iPhone to download new apps.

Maintaining Your Apple Watch

Safeguarding your Apple Watch investment is probably one of the wisest actions you should make. After all, unless you received it as a gift (lucky you), you probably spent hundreds or even many thousands of dollars on your Apple Watch, so it's a good idea to proactively protect it from damage.

Because your smartwatch is wearable, at least you don't have to worry so much about dropping it — like you would a smartphone, tablet, or laptop — but you still have steps you should take to ensure your Apple Watch runs smoothly for many years.

Avoiding water

The first tip is to be mindful of water. Remember, Apple Watch isn't waterproof. It might be splash-resistant, but you shouldn't fully submerge your wrist in water while wearing it. Keep your wrist away from the faucet when washing your hands or doing the dishes, and don't forget to take it off when you hop into the shower, climb into a bath, or step into any body of water. Your existing watch might be waterproof — and old habits die hard, as they say — so don't forget to take off Apple Watch before you do anything involving water. You really don't need to see who's texting you while you're soaking in a hot tub.

Getting caught in the rain or sweating profusely during a run are okay, says Apple, but err on the side of caution to be extra safe and leave Apple Watch behind before you go boating on a lake. Jogging with Apple Watch on a cloudy day? Don't worry about an umbrella because rain won't harm your gadget.

Avoiding extreme temps

Be cautious when using your Apple Watch in extreme temperatures. This may be a relevant consideration based on where you live or work. Are you reading this book while lying by the pool in Acapulco or Maui? Or perhaps you work in the Athabascan oil sands up in northeastern Alberta, Canada?

Apple hasn't said what the optimum environmental requirements are for Apple Watch, but assuming for a moment they're similar to its iPhone, iPod touch, iPad, and Macbook laptops, the following should be kept in mind:

- **Operating temperature:** 32° to 95° F (0° to 35° C)
- **Nonoperating temperature:** -4° to 113° F (-20° to 45° C)
- **Relative humidity:** 5 percent to 95 percent noncondensing

To be sure, however, check Apple's website or ask someone who works at an Apple Store.

Doubting its durability

While Apple advertises how strong its smartwatch is — between it solid materials, reinforced glass, and durable wristbands — try to remember you've got a sophisticated computer on your left or right wrist.

Remove the watch whenever you're doing something that could potentially damage it, such as tossing around a hardball with a child in a park or working under your car in a garage. Accidents happen, sure, but avoid the chance of impact to the area or harmful fluids from dripping onto the watch.

And then you should consider the bumps and knocks of everyday life: slamming a school locker shut, wrestling with your dog, or even putting away the dishes in drawers and cupboards. Don't be afraid to wear and use Apple Watch, but it's not immune to damage.

Considering a bumper

Just as other Apple products have countless accessories, you can bet Apple Watch will see its fair share of optional add-ons to help you get more from the wearable — and this includes protective *bumpers.*

One of the first to be announced was ActionProof's Apple Watch Bumper watch case — backed by a successful crowdfunding campaign on the Indiegogo website.

As you might suspect (or glean from the image in Figure 2-7), the $35 rubber Bumper has been designed to snugly fit and protect your Apple Watch and make it action-proof — hence, the name of the company.

Although the Bumper wraps around the body of the case, you still have access to the Digital Crown button and the Side button on the side of the watch. It also

Figure 2-7: The Apple Watch Bumper from ActionProof is designed to protect your investment.

allows for full access to the screen, backside sensors on your skin, and unob-structed use of the microphone and speaker.

Using Apple Watch responsibly

While much of the advice I dispense is common sense, you'd be surprised just how often it's forgotten or ignored. Thus, the following are some sugges-tions to being smart about your smartwatch.

Watching the road, not your wrist

Just as you shouldn't be distracted with other technology while behind the wheel — holding up a smartphone, glancing at a tablet, or fiddling with a GPS navigation device — it's critical you resist accessing Apple Watch while driving a five-ton vehicle. As the late great Jim Morrison once famously sang: "Keep your eyes on the road—your hands upon the wheel."

"But I don't have to hold a smartwatch," you say.

True, but you can still tap the screen, press one of its two buttons, look down to read something, or hold the small speaker up to your ear to listen to Siri's voice — all of which could temporarily, but fatally, distract you when you should be concentrating at the task at hand.

Of course, we all know this, but look over to your left or right while at a stop-light and you'll no doubt see someone using his or her tech gadget while in the driver seat.

It may be temping, but it can wait. The more technology we have at our fingertips, the more likely we may want to use it wherever and whenever.

Even using hands-free technology has been proven to distract drivers, so although you may be looking at the road and keeping your hands at "10 and 2" (as your driving instructor likely taught you), not exclusively focusing on your driving could be an issue.

Not here to lecture, of course, but even if this wee section reminds you about the often-overlooked dangers of distracted driving, it did its job!

Watching out for sidewalks too

Anyone who's spent time on YouTube might've seen some humorous videos of people walking down the sidewalk, oblivious to the world around them because they're staring at their smartphone, and as a result, they walk into walls or people, trip on a curb, or even fall into a manhole.

Funny? Sure. These clips prove not all of us can multitask as well as we think, especially because we can't be looking at our phone and what's in front of us at the same time.

But what you might not see on YouTube are distracted pedestrians walking into or across a road and getting hit by a vehicle. That's not so humorous, although you may be tempted to nominate these unfortunate souls for a Darwin Award, a silly online commemoration of people who perish in ridiculous ways to protect our gene pool — a nod to Charles Darwin's evolutionary theory.

One tiny little mistake in judgment and you could be seriously injured or killed — or force a car to swerve out of the way and injure passengers or other pedestrians. It's happened.

Therefore, while Apple Watch was meant to be worn and used, but mindful about your surroundings — even when you're on foot. If you want to look at, talk to, or hear your wrist-mounted companion, stop walking first.

Remembering netiquette — even when not on the Internet

Ever been to a restaurant and looked around at the other tables? You might have noticed something peculiar over the past few years: People are looking more at their mobile devices than the people they're with.

Perhaps it's an unfortunate sign of the times — be it a date night disturbed by someone checking the score of his or her favorite team or a group of friends who'd rather advertise where they are to people they're not with than appreciate those they're sitting beside.

Will the same thing happen with smartwatches? Or maybe wearable technology will be more discreet than a smartphone because you can casually glance down at your wrist while sipping a drink instead of navigating through menus on a 5.5-inch handheld?

For the sake of humanity in the digital age, we should hope technology helps rather than hinders human interaction — whether it's a couple enjoying a quiet dinner in a restaurant, kids sitting in a classroom, or business associates collaborating on a project.

Technology has a time and a place — and smartwatches are no different.

Reducing the likelihood of theft

Another take on discretion: Because many can't afford an Apple Watch, you might think twice about flaunting it on your wrist. Just as millions of smartphones are stolen in the United States each year — roughly 3.1 million in 2013, according to *Consumer Reports*, which is *nearly double* compared to 2012's numbers — you can expect many smartwatches to mysteriously disappear. In some cases, it could be from theft by force or it could be from leaving it behind (such as when traveling through security at an airport).

Many articles have been written about the dangers of tweens and teenagers showing off their newly purchased gadgets, such as smartphones and expensive headphones, so try to be a little more discreet with your Apple Watch.

The last thing you want to do is tempt fate and lose your smartwatch forever — or, worse, put your life at risk over a mere gadget.

Also, while Apple Watch doesn't hold a lot of data on it — most of it is stored on your iPhone — you still don't want your personal property falling into the wrong hands.

This might all seem a little too preachy, but I simply want to get some of these obvious — or perhaps not-too-obvious — safety, privacy, and common sense tips out of my system because I see the unspoken rules broken all the time.

Taking Advantage of Accessibility Features

In Chapter 11, I cover how to install third-party apps and tweak Apple Watch settings from inside the Apple Watch app on your iPhone. I also look at the various accessibility options and how to enable them.

But consider this section a short preview of what you can do with Apple Watch's accessibility options, which refer to features designed for those with visual or aural impairments.

Not unlike myriad options on iOS (iPhone, iPad, and iPod touch) and OS X for Mac, Apple Watch comes loaded with accessibility options you can enable in the Apple Watch app on the iPhone.

Specifically, you can enable these options:

- **VoiceOver:** A screen reader available in one of 14 languages
- **Font Adjustment:** Adjust (enlarge) fonts in many apps, such as Mail, Messages, and Settings
- **Bold Text:** Enhancing text to make it easier to read
- **Extra Large (X-Large) Watch Face:** A watch face with bigger hour/minute numbers
- **Zoom:** Easily magnify information on the screen
- **Grayscale:** Strips color from various apps and menu screens
- **Reduce Transparency:** Reduces the contrast to make text easier to read
- **On/Off Labels:** Making it easier to access settings to enable or disable features
- **Reduce Motion:** Home screen is easier to navigate
- **Mono Audio:** Sends same-channel audio to both ears or you can increase/decrease the volume in one ear
- **Prominent Haptic:** Slightly more pronounced vibration

3

Control Freak: Mastering Apple Watch's Interface and Apps

In This Chapter

▶ Recognizing the difference between a tap and a press

▶ Swiping the Apple Watch screen

▶ Exploring the Digital Crown button and the scroll feature

▶ Using the Side button

▶ Going hands-free with Siri

▶ Understanding tactile feedback: Apple Watch can tap *you*

▶ Previewing the built-in Apple Watch apps

*A*re you ready for a deeper dive into Apple Watch's controls, features, and options? That's precisely what I cover in the following pages — or digital pages if you're reading *Apple Watch For Dummies* in ebook form.

While it's unlikely you'd want to read an electronic book on Apple Watch's diminutive screen, your always-on mobile companion can do so much to help you throughout the day. This chapter explores what's possible — beginning with mastering the controls.

As with many other Apple products, the user experience is paramount, and the Cupertino, California–based company has nailed the interface once again with Apple Watch.

In other words, Apple Watch is easy to use.

After we look at using Apple Watch's screen and buttons (and microphone and speaker), I suggest a few different ways to take advantage of the watch's main features — including Glances and Notifications and the differences between the two — and then we wrap up with an overview of the built-in Apple apps.

TIP

While Apple Watch is best used while wirelessly tethered to a nearby iPhone, the watch does have 8 gigabytes (GB) of storage you can use. Well, not all of it, mind you, because the integrated storage is used by Apple for various things, including Watch OS (operating system) and parts of installed apps. But you can store up to 2 GB for offline music playlists (about 500 songs); therefore, you can leave your phone at home if you go for a jog (although Bluetooth headphones are recommended). You can also copy up to 75 megabytes worth of photos for viewing if your phone isn't around. See Chapter 9 for more on music playback.

Handling Apple Watch's Controls

This watch is on your wrist, so the main way you interface with it is with your fingertips. But you have a few different ways to do it.

Just like with your iPhone, iPod touch, and iPad, you can use your fingers on the Apple Watch screen to tap, double-tap, press, two-finger press, and swipe. The Digital Crown button and the Side button also help you access myriad features on your Apple Watch.

Tap

Tapping on something, such as an icon, is akin to hitting Enter on a computer. Or clicking the left button on a computer mouse. Tapping confirms a command, as in "Yes, I want that" — whether it's playing a song, accepting a calendar invitation, starting turn-based directions on a map, or hanging up on a completed call. As shown in Figure 3-1, tapping is the frequent method for interacting with Apple Watch.

Figure 3-1: Touch the screen with your fingertip to access apps and other content.

Speaking of taps, you can also send a *tap* to friends and loved ones to let them know you're thinking about them. Apple calls this its *Digital Touch* feature — a communications option within the Friends ring. Select someone in your Friends ring and choose a person to send a tap to, which is felt as a subtle vibration on his or her wrist via an Apple Watch (required). See Chapter 5 for more on sending taps to friends and loved ones.

Double-tap

You might not use double-tap very much, but Apple Watch does recognize this action. Once you've enabled Accessibility settings — by triple-tapping the Digital Crown button; see Chapter 2 for more on these settings — you can also have text spoken to you in a humanlike voice by double-tapping the screen. This is called *VoiceOver*. Alternatively, this feature works by simply raising your wrist. Another Accessibility option is Zoom. Quickly tap twice on the screen with two fingers for a closer look at text or images.

Press (Force Touch)

Apple Watch understands the difference between a light touch and a deep press and reacts accordingly. That is, you can quickly tap, as explained in the "Tap" section, or press with your finger and hold for a second to trigger access to a range of contextually specific controls (tied to the task at hand). Apple calls this *Force Touch*. When you use Force Touch, pressing firmly on the screen brings up additional controls in such apps as Messages, Music, and Calendar. It also lets you select different watch faces, pause or end a workout, search an address in Maps, and more. Force Touch is the most significant new sensing capability since Multi-Touch.

Two-finger press (heartbeat)

Let someone special know you're thinking about him or her by sending that person your heartbeat, as shown in Figure 3-2. The catch? He or she also needs an Apple Watch. Press two fingers on the screen at the same time and the built-in heart rate sensor records and sends your heartbeat to a loved one, who will feel it on his or her wrist. Apple calls it "a simple and intimate way to tell someone how you feel," and it's a feature not found on any other smartwatch. See Chapter 5 for more on sending your heartbeat to someone.

Swipe

Like most other mobile screens in your life — such as a smartphone, tablet, and many laptops — Apple Watch also supports on-screen swiping. If the app supports it, you can swipe around using your fingertip. Or you can call up Glances — little widgets of information — by swiping up from the bottom of the watch face. See Chapter 5 for more on Glances.

Sketch

Just as you can tap, press, and swipe on the Apple Watch screen, you can also use your finger to quickly draw something on the small display and then send it to someone else who wears an Apple Watch. Apple calls this a *sketch*. It could be a flower, heart, puppy, butterfly, wedding ring, Christmas tree, or whatever. See Figure 3-3 for an example of a sketch.

Not only will the person you send your sketch to see on his or her Apple Watch what you drew, but that person can watch your sketch come to life with animation — and then respond back with a sketch of his or her own. See Chapter 5 for more on sketches.

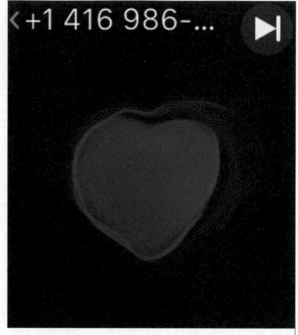

Figure 3-2: Send your heartbeat by pressing two fingers on the screen at the same time.

Digital Crown button

Apple is known for introducing new ways to interact with content, and the Digital Crown button is no exception. If the watch is worn on the left wrist, this button is on the top-right side of the Apple Watch case, and it looks like the crown on mechanical watches — used to wind the main spring and to set the time — but for the Watch OS platform, it's used primarily to magnify content on the small screen without your fingers getting in the way of content. Instead of pinching to zoom, as you would on an iPhone or iPad, twist the Digital Crown forward or backward to zoom in and out of photos or maps or to quickly scroll through contacts, songs, and more.

Keep in mind that you can flip the band around to wear the watch on your right wrist, which places the Digital Crown on the left-hand side of Apple Watch. Of course, you can keep the Side button and the Digital Crown button on the right side of the watch while wearing the watch on your right wrist, but it may not be comfortable for you to access these buttons with your left hand. But be sure to change which wrist you're wearing your watch on in the Settings area. See Chapter 11 for more on changing the watch's orientation.

At any time, you can also press the Digital Crown button to return to the Home screen (which is similar to pressing the circular Home button on an iPhone or iPad). Or press and hold the button to activate Siri. Double-pressing the Digital Crown button switches between the watch face (the one you've chosen to display) and the last app you used. It's a fast and convenient way to see the time — regardless of the app you're in. Triple-press the Digital Crown button to open the Accessibility settings on Apple Watch.

Use this list to determine how to use the Digital Crown button for a specific task:

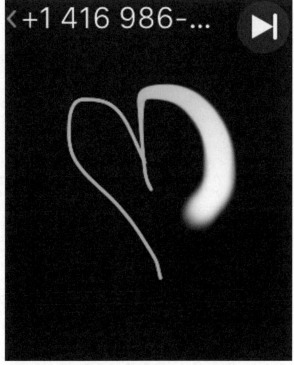

Figure 3-3: Sketch whatever you like — in your desired color — and then send it to another person's Apple Watch.

- ✔ **To return to the Home screen:** Press the Digital Crown button once to return to the watch's Home screen.

- ✔ **To return to the clock/to return to the most recent app:** Double-tap the Digital Crown button to see the clock again. Double-tap the Digital Crown button again to go back to the last app you were in.

- ✔ **To activate Siri:** Press and hold the Digital Crown button to launch your voice-activated personal assistant. Or you can just say "Hey, Siri" into your watch, followed by a question or command.

- ✔ **To zoom/scroll:** On the Home screen and in supported apps, twist the Digital Crown button forward or backward — as if you were winding your watch — to scroll through lists or zoom in on a photo, a map, the Home screen, and more.

- ✔ **To open the Accessibility settings:** Triple-tap the Digital Crown button to bring up the Accessibility options, including visual and hearing aids. See Chapter 11 for more on Accessibility settings.

Side/Power button

Apple Watch has another handy button that's located just below the Digital Crown button on the right side (if Apple Watch is worn on the left wrist). Depending on whom you ask, it's called the Side button, the Power button, or the Friends button — the latter of which refers to its primary function.

Remember, you can wear Apple Watch on the right wrist and turn around the watch case, which puts the Side button (and Digital Crown) on the left side of the watch. See Chapter 11 for more on changing the watch's orientation.

Press the Side button to bring up your Friends ring, which shows icons of your most-used contacts. You should see their initials on the ring, a photo of them (if you have one in your iPhone's Contacts for them), and their first names in the top-left corner as you scroll around the ring. Use the Digital Crown button to select a friend to call, message, send a sketch, tap, or send your heartbeat.

You'll use the Apple Watch app on your iPhone — the icon that was placed on your Home screen after downloading iOS 8.2 — to manage which friends you see when you press the Side button on your watch.

Perhaps some refer to it as a Power button because holding down this button for a couple seconds brings up a power-down screen — similar to pressing and holding the Power button on the top or side of an iPhone or iPad — and you can choose to turn it off.

Double-pressing the Side button initiates Apple Pay, allowing you to use your Apple Watch to make a purchase at a participating retailer or compatible vending machine. Once you pair your Apple Pay account with a credit or debit card, simply wave your NFC (near field communication)–enabled wristwatch over a contactless sensor to initiate the transaction. You should hear a small tone and feel a slight pulse vibration to confirm this *digital hand-shake* has been completed. Apple Pay works on Apple Watch as long the watch stays in contact with your skin. See Chapter 10 for more on Apple Pay.

Apple Watch fun fact

According to the popular 9to5Mac website, Apple's CEO Tim Cook sent a memo to employees in early April 2015 to announce that more than 1,000 Apple Watch apps had been submitted for the (not-yet-released) watch and that Apple employees could purchase the Apple Watch or Apple Watch Sport at a 50 percent discount.

The following is a summary of the Side button's features:

- **Friends:** Press the Side button once to access your Friends ring. Then, you can choose to call or message someone or, if that person also has an Apple Watch, you can send him or her your heartbeat, taps, or drawings.

- **Power:** Press and hold the Side button until you're prompted to turn off the power. You probably won't use this very much — just like you don't power down your iPhone or iPad often. But you can if you want.

- **Pay:** Double-tap the Side button to launch Apple Pay — for when you're about to buy something. Remember, Apple Pay requires skin contact to operate, so ensure the watch is snug on your wrist before you press the Side button twice to launch Apple Pay.

Going Hands-Free With Siri

Can you think of an even more natural way to interface with a smartwatch than touching it?

How about talking into it?

Apple's Siri (pronounced "sear-eee") is a voice-activated personal assistant that lets you ask questions or give a command on an iPhone, iPad, or iPod touch — and now Apple Watch. With the other iOS devices, you simply press and hold the circular Home button to ask a question.

In Chapter 7, I cover all the different ways Siri can help you master Apple Watch, but for now, I offer a quick snapshot on how to use it.

To activate Siri on your Apple Watch, follow these steps:

1. **Press and hold the Digital Crown button.**

   Siri is ready for your instructions after the short chime.

2. **Ask Siri a question or give a command.**

   You could, for example, ask "Who's winning the New York Yankees game?" In fact, you don't have to say the full team's name; therefore, asking how the "Yankees" are doing instead of the "New York Yankees" is usually fine. Siri then shows you the requested information or tells you what you asked for.

As the information is being displayed — in real time, no less — Siri also says something like "Okay, sports fans, let's have a look" or "Here you go."

3. **Press the Digital Crown button again if you want to go back to the Home screen.**

    You should then see the Apple Watch's main screen — flush with icons.

Just like with Siri on an iPhone, iPad, or iPod touch, you need an Internet connection to use Siri on Apple Watch. The requested information is sent to Apple's servers to process — like your question about the baseball score — and the information is then sent to the watch to give you the answer Your watch needs to be connected via Bluetooth or Wi-Fi to a nearby iPhone.

Vibrating Along With Apple Watch's Tactile Feedback

Apple Watch can be tapped, pressed, swiped, and spoken to. But your smartwatch can also tap *you* in the form of a light vibration. Powering this technology is what Apple calls a *Taptic Engine*.

Apple's Taptic Engine is a *linear actuator* inside Apple Watch that produces haptic feedback; in plain English, it's a slight *buzz* on your wrist whenever you receive an alert or Notification or press down on the display (like some smartphones offer). Another comparison might be a video game controller that buzzes in your hands in conjunction with what's happening on your TV screen (like your character being shot in a first-person shooter).

Not only does Apple Watch's Taptic Engine give you information without having to even look down at your wrist — such as Apple Watch telling you (based on the number of taps you felt) to turn left or right while using Apple Maps — but it also enables new and intimate ways to interact with those who also own an Apple Watch. Chapter 5 further discusses how to send a tap or your unique heartbeat to a friend or loved one.

Using Glances and Notifications

Apple Watch gives you a couple ways to glean information while on the go: Glances and Notifications.

Remember, Apple Watch isn't meant for reading lengthy websites — actually, the watch doesn't have a web browser — because it's designed for quick interactions. While they differ, Glances and Notifications give you bits of customized information — when and where you need them.

Glances

Glances are quick snippets of information you can see by swiping up from the bottom of the Apple Watch screen — perhaps how your favorite sports team is doing, weather information, or how your stock is performing.

Glances can also use time and location information if they're relevant. Although not all apps offer a Glance, you can select which Glances to display for those that do.

Glances are not scrollable. All content fits on a single screen, but tapping anywhere on a Glance opens the app to the appropriate screen. The small dots at the bottom of the screen let you scroll left and right to see other Glances. See Figure 3-4 for a Glance example.

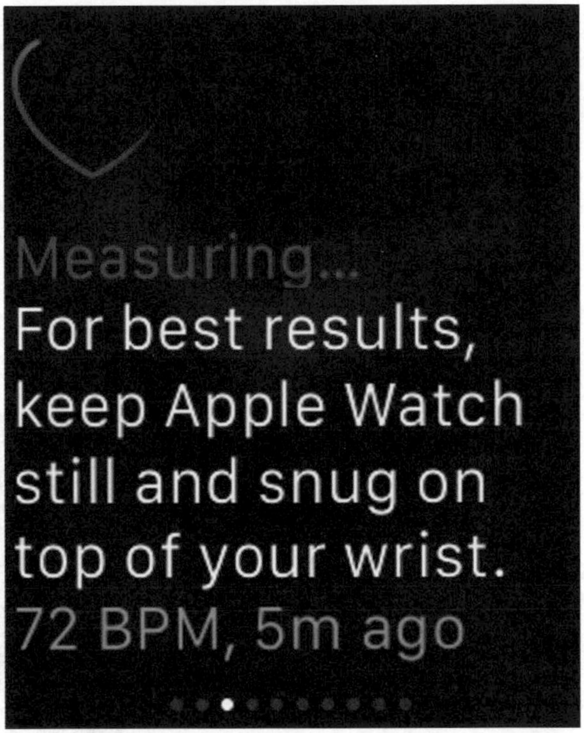

Figure 3-4: Swipe up from the bottom of the your Apple Watch's screen to see a Glance like this one.

To activate a Glance on your Apple Watch, follow these steps:

1. **Swipe up from the bottom of the clock (time) screen.**

   The Connected Glance appears first, allowing you to turn the watch to Airplane mode, make the watch silent, find your iPhone, and more.

2. **Swipe left or right within a Glance to see another Glance.**

   Swiping horizontally shows you Glances for other apps you've selected to see Glances for. For Apple's preinstalled apps, this includes Music, Heart Rate, Power, Activity, Calendar, Weather, Stocks, Maps, and World Clock.

3. **Tap anywhere on the screen to go to the app.**

   This brings you to the official app on Apple Watch to see more information than what's provided in the Glance.

Notifications

Much like Notifications on an iPhone or iPad, Notifications on Apple Watch are when an app wants you to know information at a specific time. Glances are when you ask for the information, but Notifications tell you when you need to know it.

This could be a voicemail waiting for you, a calendar appointment, a news headline from CNN, a social media Notification (someone started following you or liked your photo), your online classifieds ad was commented on, or a game wants you to come back.

Apple Watch has two kinds of Notifications:

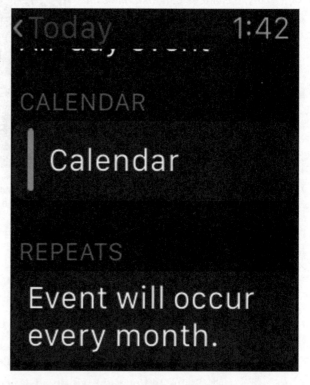

- ✔ As shown in Figure 3-5, a **Short-Look Notification** appears when a local or remote alert first arrives. It's a short look that presents a minimal amount of information to you. If your wrist is lowered, the short-look note disappears. These short looks include the app name, the icon, and the title.

- ✔ A **Long-Look Notification** appears when your wrist remains raised or if you tap the short-look interface. This provides more detailed information and more functionality (such as four action buttons for additional information), and you need to dismiss it when you're done.

Figure 3-5: Notifications on your Apple Watch can show you a bit of time- or location-relevant information.

App developers are asked by Apple to always make sure Notifications are relevant to what the user wants and to not bombard them with messages all day long. But you can turn off Notifications for any app anyway in the Apple Watch app on iPhone; see Chapter 11 for more on how to do this.

Looking at Apple Watch's Built-In Apps

Just as Apple gives you a bunch of preinstalled apps to get you going on your iPhone, iPad, iPod touch, and Mac-based computers, Apple Watch also has a number of built-in apps, including ones for keeping in touch (Phone, Messages, Email); keeping you from getting lost or finding stuff around you (Maps); and staying organized (Calendar), informed (Clock, Weather, Stocks), and entertained (Music, Photos).

I briefly listed some of these apps in Table 1-1 in Chapter 1, but here, I discuss all of them in greater depth because you're likely to rely on many of these apps. Okay, so some might not appeal to everyone, such as a stopwatch or a world clock, but they're available if and when you want them.

Phone

You no longer need to reach for your iPhone to see who's calling you. Simply glance at your wrist to see the name or number (if he or she isn't in your Contacts) and decide to take the call. Have a chat through the watch if you like or transfer it over to the iPhone. Don't want to take it? Simply cover Apple Watch with your hand to mute an incoming call. You can also place a call to someone through Apple Watch. See Chapter 5 for more on talking on your Apple Watch.

Messages

If someone sends you a text message (SMS) or an iMessage to your iPhone, Apple Watch gives you a subtle tap to let you know about it. Raise your wrist to see who wrote it and to read the message. You can reply with a preset response, send an animated emoji, dictate the response, or record and send a short audio message. See Chapter 5 for more on handling messages on your Apple Watch. See Figures 3-6 for a text message example.

Figure 3-6: Because the Apple Watch has no keyboard, you have to use your voice to dictate a reply.

Mail

While a small smartwatch screen may be more conducive for short text messages than lengthy emails, you can read your personal or professional email — as shown in Figure 3-7 — synchronized with your nearby iPhone. But you can't reply to it on Apple Watch. You can also flag emails, mark them as read or unread, or delete them. See Chapter 5 for more on reading and responding to emails on your Apple Watch.

Figure 3-7: Read your email on Apple Watch or press and hold on the screen (Force Touch) to access a few options.

Calendar

Your wrist can tell you when you've got an upcoming calendar appointment. You can set meeting reminders, accept or decline calendar invitations, and, if desired, email the organizer with a preset response. See Chapter 6 for more on Calendar options.

Alarm

Apple Watch lets you set and manage multiple alarms. You can do it by asking Siri or using the Digital Crown button to tweak the alarm time, such as a wakeup call, and you can even choose for it to be a vibrating alarm on your wrist. See Figure 3-8 for Apple Watch's Alarm app. Don't forget you can also sync your iPhone alarms to your wrist. See Chapter 4 for more on setting alarms.

Figure 3-8: Use the Alarm app to have your watch wake you up.

Stopwatch

Just like you have access to a stopwatch on your iPhone, Apple Watch offers one for your convenience — and you can set it to digital, analog, or hybrid view. Apple Watch also offers an optional graph view. See Chapter 4 for more on using the Stopwatch app on your Apple Watch.

Timer

Whether you're running around a track or cooking something in the oven, Apple Watch lets you use a timer. As the timer runs, you should see a line move around the dial to give you a sense of how much time has passed and how much is left on the timer. See Chapter 4 for more on setting timers on your Apple Watch.

World Clock

You don't need to go to a website to see the time in different cities around the world (or count on your fingers as you do the manual calculation between, say, New York and London). Launch the World Clock app to see the time in cities of your choosing. You can use your iPhone to add new locations at any time. See Chapter 4 for more on setting up the World Clock app.

Siri

Siri is a fast and convenient way to interface with your Apple Watch. In fact, nothing is more natural than using your voice, and your smartwatch responds after you say "Hey, Siri," followed by a question or command, or after pushing in and holding the Digital Crown button to activate Siri. See Chapter 7 for more on using Siri to help you do things on your Apple Watch.

Weather

Use Apple Watch to check the weather where you are or for any city in the world — the temperature and precipitation at that exact moment for the day or week ahead. See Figure 3-9 for a glimpse at the Weather app. Unless you've chosen a watch face that includes weather information, the quickest way to access that information is to ask Siri for it. The second-quickest way is to swipe up and access the Weather Glance screen. Of course, opening the app itself is the third-quickest way, but you should choose a method that works best for you. See Chapter 6 for more on the Weather app on your Apple Watch.

Figure 3-9: We love knowing the weather, and Apple Watch provides multiple ways to see it, including via the Weather app.

Stocks

Follow all the companies you have a vested interest in — or plan on buying into — with the Stocks app on your Apple Watch. The Stocks app lets you keep up with the stock market price, point and percentage, market cap, and more. All your stocks include a historical graph. See Chapter 6 for more on the Stocks app on your Apple Watch.

Activity

Activity is one of the two important fitness-related Apple Watch apps. The three Activity rings — Move, Exercise, and Stand — give you a simple yet informative glimpse into your daily activity goals and progress. The app was designed to motivate you to sit less and move more. See Figure 3-10 for the three Activity rings, and see Chapter 8 for more on the Activity app on your Apple Watch.

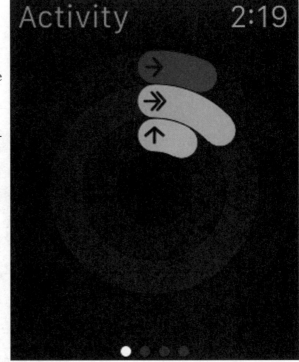

Figure 3-10: This smart, color-coded Activity app shows your daily progress.

Workout

During an exercise routine, the Workout app shows you real-time fitness information, including time, distance, calories, pace, and speed. You can choose from preset workouts, such as Running, Walking, Cycling, and others. See Figure 3-11 for a glimpse at the Workout app, and see Chapter 8 for more on the Workout app on your Apple Watch.

Maps

Whether you're trying to find a restaurant in your hometown or you feel like going on a stroll in an exotic city, your Apple Watch can give you directions based on your current location, as shown in Figure 3-12. See the fastest route, get turn-by-turn navigation instructions (including taps on your wrist when it's time to turn), or ask Siri to find local businesses. See Chapter 6 for more on the Maps app on your Apple Watch.

Photos

Those who matter to you are now just a glance away. The Photos app on Apple Watch displays your photos of loved ones, friends, pets, scenery, and other memories. Use the Digital Crown button to zoom in on individual images or swipe to browse through them one photo at a time. You can even choose photos to be loaded on the watch — even if your iPhone isn't near. See Chapter 12 for more on using the Photos app on your Apple Watch.

Remote Camera

While Apple Watch doesn't have a camera — well, not the first version of the watch anyway — it can be used as a live viewfinder for your iPhone's rear-facing iSight camera. Therefore, use your watch to see and snap a subject — essentially turning your wrist into a wireless shutter (ideal for selfies) — plus you can adjust the timer remotely. See Chapter 12 for more on using your Apple Watch to control your iPhone's camera.

Figure 3-11: The Workout app offers some exercise routines.

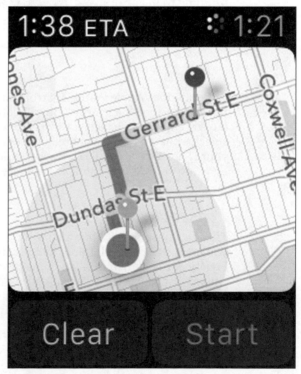

Figure 3-12: Get directions to a location, such as a local business, by using the Maps app.

Music

You can keep your iPhone tucked away in your pocket or purse and use your Apple Watch to control your music remotely. See Figure 3-13 to see what your songs — with album artwork if you've got it on your iPhone — look like on your watch. You might also want to load up your watch with a few hundred tunes to listen to when you don't have your phone with you (although Bluetooth headphones are recommended). See Chapter 9 for more on listening to music or managing your music on your Apple Watch.

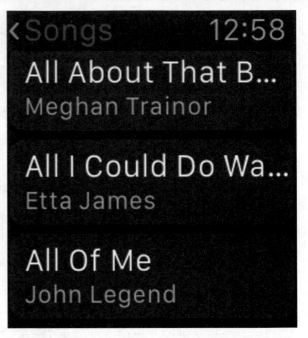

Figure 3-13: Like music? You'll love Apple Watch because it can store music you synced from your iPhone.

Remote

Not only does Apple Watch control your music on an iPhone, but it can also be used to access a nearby Apple TV box connected to your TV. Your wrist-based remote can navigate the main menu, scroll through media lists, and select what you want. Your watch's Remote app can also be used to control your iTunes library and iTunes Radio on a PC or Mac. See Chapter 9 for more on using your Apple Watch as a remote control.

Passbook

This handy app for iPhone also works well on Apple Watch. Passbook helps you keep track of such things as boarding passes, movie or theater tickets, loyalty cards, and more —and time-based alerts let you know when you should or can use them. When you shop with Apple Pay, this app also lets you choose which credit or debit cards to use. See Chapter 10 for more on using Apple Pay with your Apple Watch as well as more about Passbook.

Settings

The Settings app for Apple Watch lets you enable or disable a number of settings, including Airplane mode (turning off all wireless radios), Bluetooth, and Do Not Disturb. This app also lets you mute your watch in case you don't want to hear any sounds emit from it. Lost your iPhone under the cushions? Your Apple Watch can make your iPhone *ping* loudly so you can hear it and find it. See Chapter 11 for more on the Settings app on your Apple Watch.

Part II
Just the Tasks, Ma'am

In this part . . .

✔ Learn about all ten Apple Watch faces as well as how to customize them and add complications to them. Then, you can discover how to turn your Apple Watch into an alarm, stopwatch, and timer.

✔ Explore the Friends ring and how to add contacts to your Apple Watch. Then, find out how to use your Apple Watch to make and take phone calls, send and receive text messages, and read and manage your email. You can also learn how to send your actual heartbeat to a friend or loved one.

✔ Turn your Apple Watch into a miniature media outlet by adding Glances and Notifications on topics you care about, such as the current weather, stock market performance, breaking news, live sports scores, and more. Then, learn how to keep track of appointments with the Calendar app and how to use your Apple Watch as a GPS via the Maps app.

4

It's About Time: Learning How to Set Watch Faces, Alarms, Timers, and More

*A*pple Watch is a watch after all, so chances are you'll use it a lot to tell time. But unlike a traditional analog watch or even most digital watches, Apple Watch lets you choose the face you want. This way, you can select what you'd like to see and how you'd like the information displayed.

This chapter looks at the ten watch faces you can choose from and customize so you can truly make Apple Watch your own as well as the different ways to access the watch face on Apple Watch. I also review other time-related apps preinstalled by Apple, including the World Clock, Stopwatch, Timer, and Alarm apps.

Looking at the Built-In Watch Faces

Why be stuck with only one watch face when you can have multiple ones to choose from?

That's one of the reasons why people like a smartwatch. Because you've got a screen that can show virtually anything on it, you can go with a classic analog face (yes, with moving hands!), a digital watch face (just numbers), a hybrid of the two, or even one with animation on it.

It's a breeze to change these watch faces whenever you like — see the "Choosing From the Various Watch Faces" section later in this chapter — and without having to open up the Apple Watch app on your iPhone. By default, your watch face is one called *Modular*, which is a basic digital clock, along with an area for the date, calendar events, temperature, and a world clock if you like.

By the way, while you've got many watch faces to choose from and customize, Apple hints in its Apple Watch User Guide (`http://help.apple.com/watch`) that it may add more options in the future. It says: "Apple Watch includes a variety of watch faces, any of which you can customize to suit you. Check frequently for software updates; the set of watch faces that follows might differ from what you see on your Apple Watch."

Plus, in the Apple Watch App Store, you can download many more watch faces — in the form of an app — to truly make Apple Watch uniquely yours (such as a virtual Cuckoo Clock app). But to get you going, Apple has installed ten built-in watch faces.

Nothing gets past Apple fans

Apple Watch offers ten different faces: Astronomy, Chronograph, Color, Mickey Mouse, Modular, Motion, Simple, Solar, Utility, and X-Large. Each one can be customized with different customizations and complications — both of which are discussed in this chapter. But when Apple Watch was first announced in fall 2014, two other watch faces were advertised, as noted by a few Apple fanboys on social media. Curiously missing at launch are the Photo and Timeless faces, which both show a photo behind the time. Perhaps it eats up too much power? Too bad because they looked cool.

Astronomy

Apple says it worked with astrophysicists to create this visually striking watch face, as shown in Figure 4-1. It shows the time and date at the top of the screen, but you can turn the Digital Crown button to see Earth's rotation, the moon phases, and even the entire solar system — all accurately displayed in time. Consider it a throwback to the oldest way to tell time: with stars, planets, and our moon.

Figure 4-1: The Astronomy watch face.

Chronograph

Resembling an analog stopwatch, the Chronograph watch face has one main analog clock — with hour, minute, and second hands — but also two additional smaller hands: one for total time and a second for lap times, as shown in Figure 4-2. These secondary faces are very customizable too. You can also choose to place additional information in each of the four corners, which is explained in greater depth later in this chapter in the "Differentiating Between Customizations and Complications" section.

Figure 4-2: The Chronograph watch face.

Color

By twisting the Digital Crown button, you can choose a watch face color that suits your outfit, style, or mood. This classic analog face can be as minimalist or as busy as you like based on the number of complications you select. See Figure 4-3 for the Color watch face.

Figure 4-3: The Color watch face.

Mickey Mouse

The classic Mickey Mouse analog watch — shown in Figure 4-4 — has been reinvented for Apple Watch. Mickey's arms move around the dial as they point to the correct hour and minute while his foot taps every second. Expect the Mickey Mouse face to be a fan favorite among Apple Watch wearers.

Figure 4-4: The Mickey Mouse watch face.

Oh, Mickey, you're so fine

This isn't the first time Apple has put Mickey Mouse on its gadgets. Apple launched a new iPod nano back in the fall of 2011 — and with it came 16 new clock faces, including ones with beloved Disney characters Mickey Mouse and Minnie Mouse.

And did you know the original Mickey Mouse watch debuted back in 1933 and became an instant hit? In fact, it saved the cash-strapped Ingersoll company from bankruptcy (like with many others companies, the Great Depression hurt Ingersoll's business considerably). The Mickey Mouse watch originally sold for $2.98 at Macy's and then $2.69 at Sears, Roebuck & Company.

Modular

As the name suggests, this digital watch face — shown in Figure 4-5 — allows for the most number of complications out of all watch faces, which gives you a ton of extra information at a glance. The interface can be as clean or cluttered as you see fit.

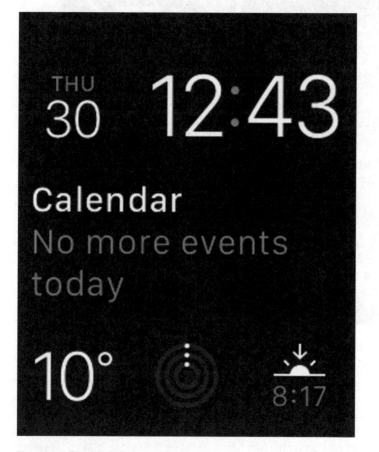

Figure 4-5: The Modular watch face.

Motion

Apple Watch fans are going to love this one. This watch face displays a different animated image every time you raise your wrist. Based on the theme you choose, raise your wrist and you might see a butterfly slowly fluttering its wings — as shown in Figure 4-6 — or a flower blooming.

Figure 4-6: The Motion watch face.

Attention to detail

Apple always goes above and beyond. Some of these objects for the Motion watch face were video-recorded, such as the jellyfish (at 300 frames per second), while others — such as the blooming flowers — were created using stop-motion time-lapse photos. Apple says a single flower took more than 285 hours and 24,000 shots to photograph.

Simple

The most minimalist of all Apple Watch faces, Simple — as the name implies — offers a straightforward yet elegant face with analog hands for minute, hour, and second, as shown in Figure 4-7. A single number tells you the day of the month. But as with all other watch faces, you can adjust the amount of detail with the Digital Crown button.

Figure 4-7: The Simple watch face.

Solar

Along with showing you the time digitally, Solar lets you see the sun's position in the sky above — along its arc from sunrise to sunset, as shown in Figure 4-8. The small white sun changes position in the sky based on the time of day or you can follow its path over time as you twist the Digital Crown button.

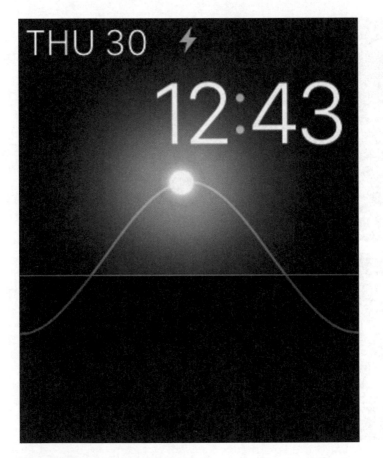

Figure 4-8: The Solar watch face.

Utility

The most straightforward and practical face out of the bunch, Utility shows you a classic analog watch face but with plenty of space in the corners for extra information, such as the world clock, the timer, or a calendar appointment, as shown in Figure 4-9.

Figure 4-9: The Utility watch face.

X-Large

As you might expect with a name like X-Large, this watch face shows a very large digital clock with the hour on the top of the screen and the minutes on the bottom, as shown in Figure 4-10. While the background is black, you can adjust the color to your liking — perhaps to match an outfit you're wearing.

Figure 4-10: The X-Large watch face.

Can Apple make the watch relevant again?

Smartwatch naysayers claim that many of us have moved on from the watch and now rely on our phones to tell time. Therefore, even a so-called "smart" watch won't appeal to that many people, but once you have the time on your wrist, it's certainly more convenient than pulling out that phone from your back pocket or purse.

"Time" will tell if Apple and other smartwatch makers can make the watch relevant again — I'd argue the wrist is indeed coveted real estate to add some technology to — of which telling time is just the beginning.

That said, Apple's CEO Tim Cook made it very clear Apple Watch should not only be a functional timepiece but also an accurate one. For more on time accuracy, see www.dummies.com/extras/applewatch.

Choosing From the Various Watch Faces

One of the first things you might do with Apple Watch is to choose one of the ten watch faces provided and then customize it to your liking — perhaps with complications. And it's super easy to change faces and make those optional changes — both of which you can do right on the watch itself.

To select a specific watch face for your Apple Watch, follow these steps:

1. **When viewing the default (Modular) watch face, press and hold the screen.**

   This enables Force Touch and launches the Faces gallery.

2. **Swipe left or right to select a clock face you like and then tap the center of the watch face you want to use for time.**

3. **Tap Customize near the bottom of the screen to personalize the face.**

   The small white dots on the top of the screen tell you how many different customization screens are available for this face. You can change whatever is in the green outline, as shown in Figure 4-11.

4. **Twist the Digital Crown button to customize the screen. When you like what you see — for example, changing the color of the hands or text or adding a second hand — swipe to the left to go to the next customization screen. I cover customizations in greater depth in the "Differentiating Between Customizations and Complications" section.**

Figure 4-11: Whatever is highlighted in green can be customized by twisting the Digital Crown button.

Twist the Digital Crown button to make your selection once again. Repeat this step until you've gone through all the customization screens — perhaps choosing color and extra time information. Typically, the last customization page is for complications.

5. **Tap the green areas that can be added to your watch screen, as shown in Figure 4-12, and then twist the Digital Crown button to select what you're happy with.**

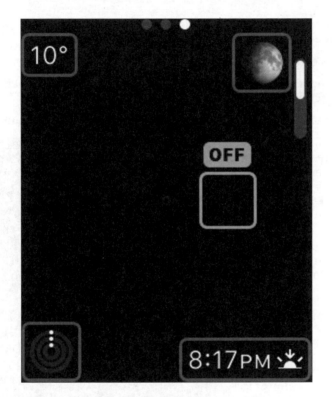

Figure 4-12: Don't worry if you don't like your choices because you can go in at any time and tweak them again.

Repeat the process by tapping the other areas of the face you want to change, which will vary by which watch face you go with. Remember, you won't have the same options for all watch faces.

6. **Press the Digital Crown button when you're done customizing your watch face.**

   This confirms you've finished with your options and are ready to see your customized watch face.

7. **Tap the center of the screen to confirm your changes.**

   After you've set your watch face, don't forget you can tap on each of the complications — such as weather or stock quotes, as shown in Figure 4-13 — which are discussed in further detail in the "Differentiating Between Customizations and Complications" section.

That's it! That wasn't so difficult, right?

Figure 4-13: After you've completed your customization, this is the watch face you might see when you raise your wrist.

Differentiating Between Customizations and Complications

It's important to understand that all the watch faces support various tweaks you can make to help your Apple Watch feel even more personal. Apple divides these personalized changes into two main categories: customizations and complications.

Customizations

Each watch face includes customizations you can perform, such as changing the watch to show additional information (such as specific minute, second, or millisecond detail) and changing the color of the watch hands (perhaps to match your outfit). You can make changes for each face, but what you can change varies by face style. See Figures 4-14 and 4-15 for customization examples.

Figure 4-14: Customize the look of your watch face by adjusting the amount of information you want to see.

Complications

When customizing your watch's face, one of your options is to add additional information to the screen — usually in up to four corners or at the bottom part of the screen. This may include upcoming calendar alerts, an alarm, the current moon phase, the weather, the day's sunrise and sunset times, a timer or stopwatch, your current activity, the world clock, and stock quotes. When customizing the watch, simply touch highlighted parts of the watch face to make your selection. Be aware, however, that some watch faces offer more room for complications than others. When you tap on the piece of information provided, such as the weather, Apple Watch opens up the corresponding app for a deeper dive.

The word *complications*, by the way, is a horological term that refers to any clock feature that goes beyond the display of hours and minutes.

TIP

You can still tell the time on Apple Watch if the battery is low. Your watch automatically goes into the Power Reserve mode when your battery drops below a certain percentage or you can activate this mode manually by opening the Settings app on Apple Watch. You should still be able to see the time for up to 48 hours, according to Apple.

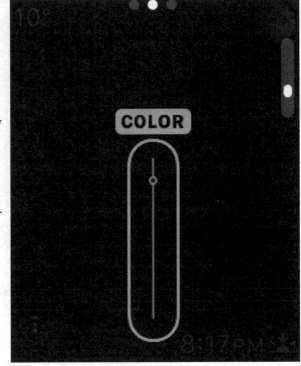

Figure 4-15: A look at tweaking the color of the hands via the Digital Crown button.

Looking closer at ten complications

You can choose one of ten complications — see Figures 4-16 and 4-17 for examples — to add to your Apple Watch face (if it's supported):

7:00

✔ **Alarm:** As the name suggests, you can set an alarm, such as that dreaded wakeup call, and see what time it's set for.

14:59

✔ **Timer:** Set one or more timers right on your Apple Watch and you should see the timer icon count down to zero from your set time (minutes/hours). No more burnt cookies.

00:00

✔ **Stopwatch:** Ready, set, go! Right from the watch face, you can start and stop a digital stopwatch. As you likely know, numbers climb up from zero over time and can be reset to start again.

LON 5:09

✔ **World Clock:** Have relatives in another country? Work associates on a different continent? You can set a secondary clock on your watch face and you'll see an abbreviated name for a location (such as PAR for Paris) and the correct time there.

Figure 4-16: What can you choose to place on your watch face? A lot, as you can see here.

7:10

✔ **Sunrise/Sunset:** While it's also the name of a famous song in *Fiddler on the Roof*, this complication lets you see when the sun is set to go down and rise the next day.

✔ **Moon Phase:** Werewolves, beware! This complication shows you how much of the moon will be visible that night, such as crescent, half, or full.

MON
9

✔ **Calendar:** See when your next appointment is and what it's about by syncing information from your iPhone's Calendar app. Hopefully, it's nothing embarrassing your colleagues might accidentally see, such as "2 p.m.: Proctologist Appointment"!

72°

✔ **Weather:** Without even having to open an app, your Apple Watch can tell you the weather outside based on what city you're in (or another city of your choosing). You can choose to see the information in Fahrenheit or Celsius. Ideal for Canadians, eh?

AAPL
+.94

✔ **Stocks:** Should you celebrate or bite your nails? The Stocks complication shows you real-time quotes based on the publicly traded companies that matter to you.

✔ **Activity:** Get a quick idea of how active you've been throughout the day. The three rings show your actual level of physical activity and how much of your daily goal you've accomplished. Lazy types might be tempted to throw the watch out, but it won't berate you.

Figure 4-17: An example of a kind of complication you can add to a watch face.

Accessing Time on Apple Watch

If you've mastered how to select a watch face and customize it — and even if you still need to do those things — you might want to know how to access the clock on your Apple Watch. It's probably the screen you're going to see the most, so it's something we need to cover, don't ya think?

It's actually quite easy — even if you're in another app.

By default, Apple Watch shows you the clock screen when you raise your wrist. Therefore, you need not do anything if you like this setup. The screen stays on for about four to six seconds — whether you look at it or not — and then goes back to sleep again (presumably to save on power).

If you tap the screen or press the Digital Crown button or the Side button, however, the screen stays on for about 15 to 17 seconds before fading to black.

Want to see something other than the time when you raise your wrist? No problem. Grab your iPhone because you need it to change the default setting to one other option, and then follow these steps:

1. **From the Apple Watch app on your iPhone, choose My Watch⇨Settings ⇨General.**

   Near the bottom of the screen, you should see the words Activate on Wrist Raise, as shown in Figure 4-18.

2. **If you like seeing the time when you raise your wrist, do nothing. But change it to Resume Previous Activity instead of Clock Face if you'd prefer to see the last app used when looking at your wrist.**

   Resume Previous Activity is another way of seeing the last app you were in. You can also do this in the Settings app on the Apple Watch itself. Tap Activate on Wrist Raise and then change it from Clock Face to Resume Previous Activity. Perhaps Apple will give you more options in a future update, but these are your only two for now.

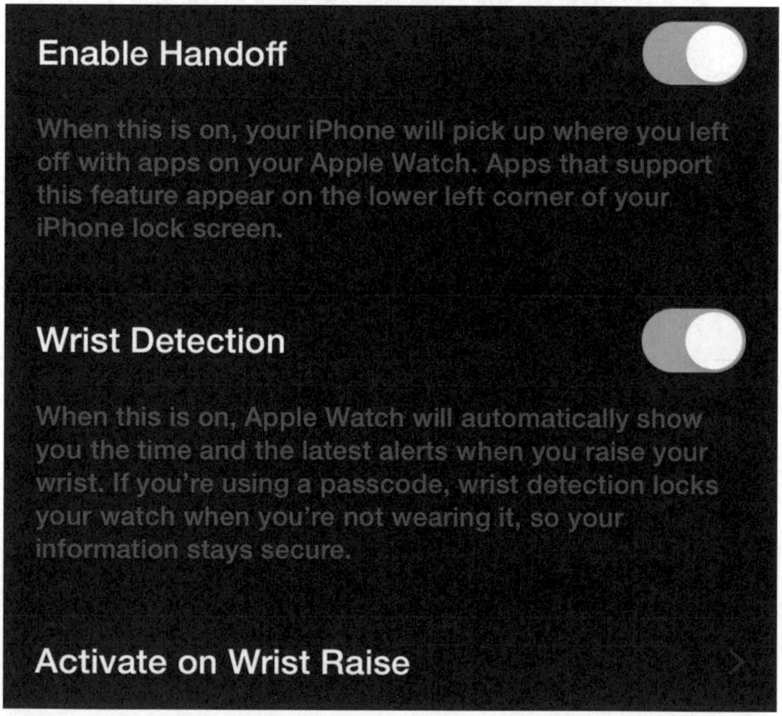

Enable Handoff

When this is on, your iPhone will pick up where you left off with apps on your Apple Watch. Apps that support this feature appear on the lower left corner of your iPhone lock screen.

Wrist Detection

When this is on, Apple Watch will automatically show you the time and the latest alerts when you raise your wrist. If you're using a passcode, wrist detection locks your watch when you're not wearing it, so your information stays secure.

Activate on Wrist Raise

Figure 4-18: The Apple Watch app on iPhone. Here, you can enable and disable various Apple Watch functions.

Not entirely sure what Last Used App means? If you were in, say, the Calendar app or Messages app and you lower your wrist to get on with your day, you can choose to see that app first whenever you raise your wrist again.

You can also easily see the time whenever you're in any app (as further described in Chapter 3). Simply double-press the Digital Crown button and you immediately see the watch faces appear on your screen. Now double-press the Digital Crown button again and you return to the last app you were in.

You have a third way to get the time on your Apple Watch — and you don't even need to look at your wrist at all. Can you guess what it is? Give up? You can ask Siri what time is it. Press and hold the Digital Crown button and ask "What time is it?" or simply say "Time." Alternatively, you can ask "What time is it in ____ (and name a city around the world)"? You can also raise your wrist and say into your wrist "Hey, Siri, what time is it?" See Chapter 7 for more on using Siri to help you complete tasks with your Apple Watch.

Accessing World Time

Some people like to know what time it is in another part of the globe. You know, in case you want to Skype or Facetime with someone and you're not sure if it's the middle of the night where that person is.

Whether it's for personal or professional reasons, a world clock could be a handy thing to have — and your Apple Watch can help you with that.

Earlier in Chapter 4 — in the "Differentiating Between Customizations and Complications" section — I discussed adding a world clock as a complication to an existing watch face, but it's also something you can view on your own.

To use the World Clock app on your Apple Watch, follow these steps:

1. **Press the Digital Crown button to go to the Home screen.**

   Regardless of the app you're in, you should see the screen with all the small icons on it once you press the Digital Crown button. If you don't see what you want at first glance, swipe your finger around to view other bubble-shaped icons.

2. **Tap the World Clock app.**

   The app launches full screen and you should see the time in another city. If you haven't added another city yet, Apple Watch might say "No World Clocks," such as it does on an iPhone.

3. **If you have more than one city selected, you can swipe left or right to navigate between them.**

   The top right of the screen is your local time. But then you should see the remote city highlighted by an orange dot on a map, the name of the city, the time there, the time zone, and sunrise and sunset information, as shown in Figure 4-19.

4. **If you don't have any locations installed or if you'd like to add more (or remove one), open the Settings tab on your iPhone's Apple Watch app (under General). When you've made your selection, you can just exit the app.**

   Of course, you can also ask Siri for this information, such as "What time is it in Warsaw?" or "What time will the sun rise in Tokyo?" See Chapter 7 for more tasks Siri can help you with.

Figure 4-19: When you launch the World Clock app, your screen should look similar to this.

Taking Control: Alarms, Stopwatches, and Timers — Oh My!

Alarms, timers, and stopwatches are great tools to have with you. And because you're wearing Apple Watch on your wrist, you have access to them wherever life takes you.

Alarms

Apple Watch lets you easily set an alarm, such as a 7 a.m. wakeup call, viewed in either an analog or digital display. To change between digital and analog, press firmly on the screen and then tap Customize. Swipe left until you see the alarm face you like.

To set up a new alarm on Apple Watch, follow these steps:

1. **Press the Digital Crown button to go to the Home screen.**

2. **Tap the Alarm app.**

   This launches the Alarm app. From this screen, you can view, manage, and edit multiple alarms with your fingertip.

   To set an alarm with Siri, press and hold the Digital Crown button to activate Siri or simply raise your wrist and say "Hey, Siri," followed by "Set an alarm for ____ (date and time)." You can also say "Wake me up at ____ (time of day)" or even "Wake me up in ____ (minutes or hours)."

   Siri confirms the time and shows it to you on the watch's screen, as shown in analog mode in Figure 4-20. It's totally fine to have multiple alarms.

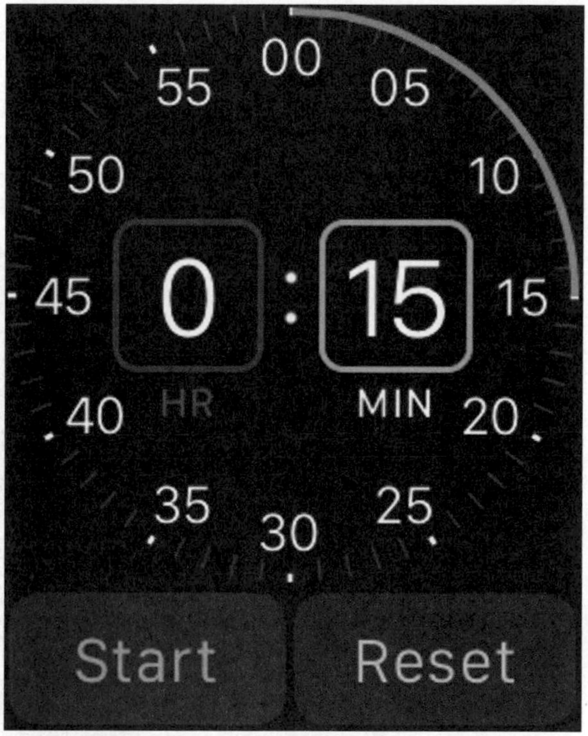

   Figure 4-20: The analog mode of the Alarm screen. Set your desired time using the Digital Crown button.

3. **To set your alarm time, twist the Digital Crown button to adjust the hours and minutes and then tap Set. Figure 4-21 shows an alarm setting.**

   Your alarm is now set. You can uncheck ones you no longer need. You can also press and hold the Apple Watch screen in the Alarm app to bring up options, including alarm repeats (such as for weekdays). When the alarm goes off, you can tap Snooze or Dismiss.

Figure 4-21: It's a cinch to adjust your alarm time — even if you're half asleep and fumbling to set a wakeup call.

Your iPhone alarms can also be synchronized with your Apple Watch. This happen automatically by default, but you can also go into your Apple Watch app on an iPhone and tap My Watch and then Settings to disable this feature.

Stopwatches

You don't need to be an Olympian runner to appreciate a stopwatch, which measures the ascending passage of time. Whatever the reason you'd like to know how much time has elapsed, the Stopwatch app is what you need — and it's fully customizable too.

That is, the Stopwatch app on Apple Watch lets you see information in a digital, analog, or hybrid view or even in a graph that shows a real-time average of your lap times. See Figure 4-22 for a look at the hybrid view.

To use the Stopwatch app on Apple Watch, follow these steps:

1. **Press the Digital Crown button to go to the Home screen.**

2. **Tap the Stopwatch app.**

   This launches the Stopwatch app. You can also raise your wrist and then say "Hey, Siri, Stopwatch" or press and hold the Digital Crown button to initiate Siri.

Figure 4-22: You can choose a hybrid of analog and digital, as shown here.

3. **Tap the green Start button in the lower left, as shown in Figure 4-23, to start the stopwatch.**

   Whether you're in analog, digital, or hybrid view (which you can change in the Settings area of the iPhone's Apple Watch app, as discussed in Chapter 11), you should see the time scroll by.

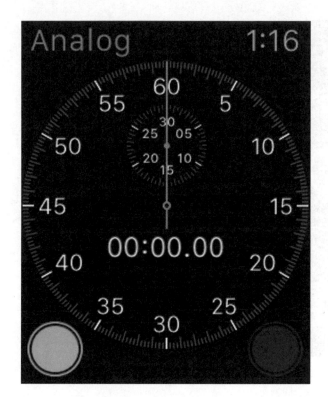

Figure 4-23: The Stopwatch app in action.

4. **Press the red Stop button in the lower-right corner of the screen to stop the stopwatch.**

   Don't worry if you accidentally close the app without taking note of your time because it's still there when you open up the app again.

5. **Tap the Lap button in the lower-right corner of the app if you want to see graphed averages of lap times.**

   Joggers and runners might appreciate this added historical information, as shown in Figure 4-24.

Timers

The Timer app lets you keep track of events you want, well, timed. While the Stopwatch app measures the ascending passage of time, the Timer app offers the descending passage of time — from a preset starting point, such as 45 minutes.

Figure 4-24: The Stopwatch app offers a historical/graphical look of your lap times.

As with the other time-related apps, you can choose to read a digital or analog countdown.

To use the Timer app on your Apple Watch, follow these steps:

1. **Press the Digital Crown button to go to the Home screen.**

2. **Tap the Timer app.**

   This launches the Timer app. Alternatively, you can say "Hey, Siri, Timer" or press and hold the Digital Crown button to activate Siri and then say "Timer."

3. **Twist the Digital Crown button to select the starting time.**

   You start with the hour setting, but press the Digital Crown button to go to the minute setting and then press the Digital Crown button again when you're done. Review what you selected for a start time, such as 30 minutes or an hour and 15 minutes.

4. **Tap the green Start button on the lower-left side to initiate the timer.**

   As the timer runs, an orange line moves around the dial in clockwise fashion to help give you a visual sense for how much time has passed (and how much is left). See Figure 4-25 for a look at the Timer app in all its glory.

5. **When you're done, press the Reset button in the lower-right corner of the Apple Watch screen.**

   Pressing Reset rolls back the timer to all zeros, making it ready for next time. If you no longer need the timer, press the Digital Crown button.

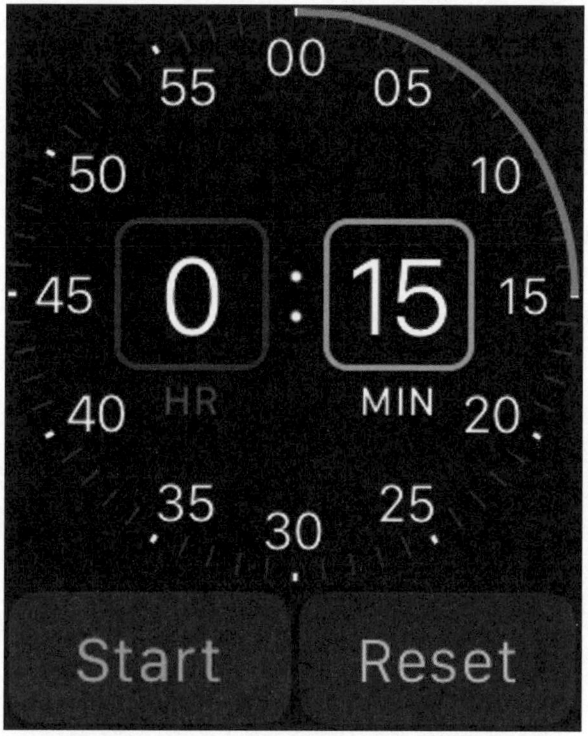

Figure 4-25: The analog and digital hybrid screen of the Timer app.

5

Keep in Touch: Using Apple Watch for Calls, Texts, Emails, and More

In This Chapter

▶ Mastering your Friends ring

▶ Accepting and placing calls on your Apple Watch

▶ Handing off calls to your iPhone

▶ Receiving and sending messages

▶ Receiving and managing emails

▶ Sending taps, sketches, and heartbeats via Apple Watch

Apple Watch isn't used just for information — such as the time, the weather, and sports scores — but it's also ideal for keeping in touch with those who matter.

In other words, your smartwatch isn't just about knowledge; it's also about communication. That's precisely what this chapter is all about.

On one hand, if you can pardon the pun, you've got the same familiar ways to connect as you can on your iPhone, which is also required for most of them too. Specifically, your Apple Watch can place and accept calls as well as send messages and emails. While Apple Watch was designed for quick interactions, it supports many of the same chatting features as your smartphone.

But it can also be used to reach out to others in new and unique ways, such as sending someone a tap or your heartbeat, which he or she will feel on his or her wrist (if that person is wearing an Apple Watch, which he or she must to feel these sensations). You can also send a finger-drawn sketch to someone special. Of course, the main way to initiate any correspondence is through your Friends ring.

Using the Friends Ring

Anyone remember when BlackBerry smartphones let you assign a speed dial to your favorite contacts? You could assign a contact to a letter on your phone's keyboard, such as "K" for "Kellie," and it immediately called the person for you. Genius.

Apple Watch offers something similar — nay, better — that also pulls up those nearest and dearest to you so you can contact them in a number of different ways. Apple calls this *Friends*. Simply press the Side button to call up this list anytime, which is presented as a ring (or wheel, if you prefer) so you can scroll through and select someone to reach out to.

Before you can call up your Friends ring on Apple Watch, however, you need to assign up to 12 people from your iPhone's Contacts.

To add people to your Friends ring on your Apple Watch, follow these steps:

1. **Open the Apple Watch app on your iPhone and then select My Watch.**

   The My Watch tab is in the lower-left corner of the app.

2. **Tap Friends, which opens a screen, as shown in Figure 5-1, that lets you add up to a dozen people to your Friends ring on your watch.**

   Don't worry if you don't want to add all 12 right away. You can always add more later on or even replace someone if you like.

3. **Tap Add Friend and then use the search window to find people in your Contacts.**

   When you're done, simply leave the app and these contacts are automatically synced to your watch's Friends ring.

To contact someone via your Friends ring on your Apple Watch, follow these steps:

1. **Tap the Side button on your Apple Watch — no matter which app you're in.**

   This pulls up your Friends ring — as shown in Figure 5-2 — which shows you people you like to communicate with.

2. **Twist the Digital Crown button to select someone to contact.**

   Twist the Digital Crown button up and down to navigate around the ring — clockwise or counterclockwise, respectively. You don't need to press the Digital Crown button to select the person. Just wait a second and you should see an expanded view of his or her initials and/or face.

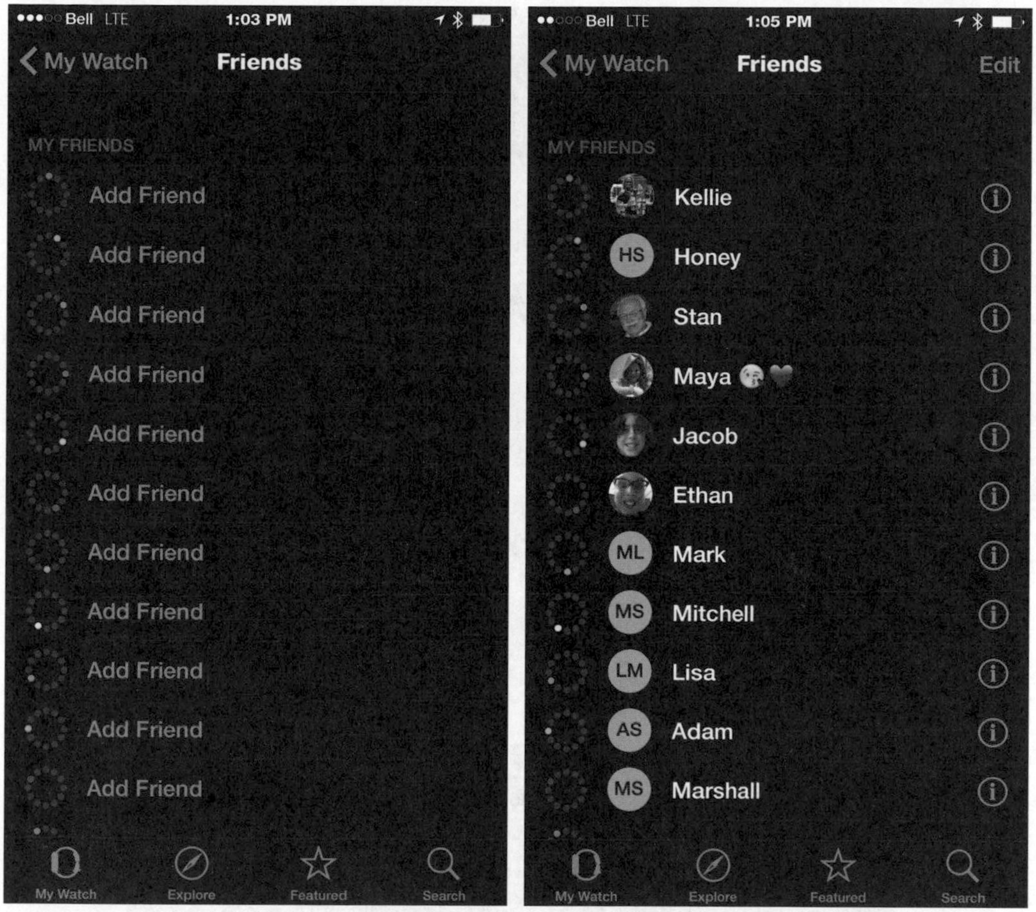

Figure 5-1: This is what it should look like when you populate each entry with people from your contacts.

To see a person's face in your Friends ring, you need to have a photo of him or her in your Contacts app on your iPhone — although it didn't always work in my testing.

Select how you'd like to contact the person: Call, Message, or, if that person has an Apple Watch, via Digital Touch.

As shown in Figure 5-3, the small icons are a phone (to call), a speech bubble (to message), or a hand with forefinger extended (Digital Touch). In the "Sending Taps, Sketches, and Heartbeats via Apple Watch" section, I cover the different ways to use Digital Touch, such as sending some vibrating taps, your heartbeat, or an animated sketch. If you can't wait to read about that fun stuff, you can skip right to the end of this chapter.

Figure 5-2: Use the Digital Crown button to select someone on this ring or simply tap the desired person on the screen.

The Friends screen is a fast and convenient way to initiate a connection to a dozen of your closest friends, family members, or coworkers. What about reading email messages from these people? See the section "Receiving and Managing Emails on Apple Watch" to learn how.

Figure 5-3: You can contact someone via a call, a message, or Digital Touch, respectively.

Accepting and Placing a Call on Apple Watch

If you want to be like Dick Tracy and take calls on your wrist, Apple Watch lets you do just that. Or make a call by pressing the Digital Crown button and asking Siri to call someone. Whether you initiate the call or accept it, as long as you have your iPhone nearby, you can chat through your smartwatch's microphone and hear the other person through the small speaker.

Using your Apple Watch to chat with others can be handled via Bluetooth technology with your nearby iPhone — up to a few dozen feet away — or even farther than that over Wi-Fi. As long as your iPhone is connected to the same wireless network — such as at home or at the office — your watch rings at the same time as your phone, and you can choose which one to answer (or not).

Incoming calls

This is the easy one.

If a call comes in to your phone number, your Apple Watch rings just like your iPhone — unless you choose to disable that feature in the Apple Watch app on your iPhone, which you can learn how to do in Chapter 11.

Assuming you didn't mess with the default settings, you hear your ring tone emanate through your watch's speaker and see a screen pop up with the name of the person calling (or just a phone number if that person isn't in your Contacts).

Tap the big green Answer icon in the bottom right of your watch's screen to answer the call. Say hello.

If you don't want to answer the call, tap the big red (Hang Up) icon in the lower left of your Apple Watch. Alternatively, you can swipe up from the bottom of your watch to send a preset message back to the person trying to reach you, such as "Call you later," "In a meeting," or "I'm driving." Just make sure that call is coming from a mobile phone or else the caller may not see it.

Figure 5-4 shows a couple preset messages you can send back if you're unable (or unwilling) to speak.

You can also customize these preset replies by going into the Settings ⇨ Messages area of the Apple Watch app on your iPhone; see Chapter 11 for more on doing this.

But as infomercial guru Ron Popeil once famously said: "But wait — there's more!"

You can also choose to transfer the call to your iPhone, a Bluetooth headset, or a car's speakerphone. See the "Handing Off a Call to Your iPhone or via Bluetooth" section for more on this.

Figure 5-4: If you have an incoming call you can't take, you can choose a desired reply, which you can customize in the Apple Watch app on your iPhone.

If you want to stop your wrist from ringing — perhaps you're in a crowded elevator and you're getting dirty looks from someone — you can silence an incoming call by simply covering Apple Watch with your other hand.

You can try to cover it with the same hand the watch is on, but that may prove a tad difficult.

The Phone app screen on Apple Watch also lets you mute your microphone by tapping the microphone with a slash through it (in case you don't want other participants in a conference call to hear you sneeze!). At the top of the watch screen, you can also increase or decrease the volume coming through the phone's speaker.

Outgoing calls

While certainly not difficult, outgoing calls through your Apple Watch requires a little more work. And that's assuming you actually *want* to make a call through your wrist.

A few considerations: It may not be too comfortable to hold up your wrist for an extended period of time; the quality of the call won't be as good as on a phone; your conversations may be heard because it's a speakerphone (unless you're wearing a Bluetooth headset); and, oh, you might look a little silly too.

The Apple website also suggests you might not want to talk for long on Apple Watch anyway: "Use the built-in speaker and microphone for quick chats, or seamlessly transfer calls to your iPhone for longer conversations."

With that in mind, you can place a call on your Apple Way in a few ways:

- **First approach:** Press the Digital Crown button to go to your Home screen and then tap the Phone icon, which is green and with a white phone in the middle. Go ahead and dial the number.

- **Second approach:** Press the Side button to bring up your Friends ring and then twist the Digital Crown button to find someone to call. Tap the Call icon for a given contact, as shown in Figure 5-5.

- **Third approach:** Lift your wrist and say "Hey, Siri" into your watch, followed by "Call ____ (person's name)" (if that person is in your phone's Contacts list) or "Dial ____ (phone number)." Or you can press and hold the Digital Crown button to activate Siri. Or you can just say "Hey, Siri, make a call" and wait for it to ask you to name someone or provide a number, as shown in Figure 5-6.

Which way do you like best? You can always revert back to smoke signals or Morse code if all this technology is making your head spin.

Figure 5-5: You can also place a call from within the Friends ring. Tap the handset icon (on the left).

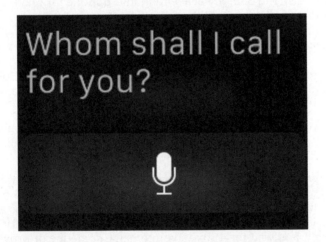

Figure 5-6: The fastest way to make a call? Use Siri to dial a contact or phone number.

If you ever want to turn the Apple Watch screen off or silence any sounds coming from it, simply cup your hand over the face and it should go dark and silent.

Handing Off a Call to Your iPhone or via Bluetooth

You probably don't want to talk for long periods of time through your Apple Watch — if only because it eats up the battery. The solution to this is wirelessly handing off the call to your iPhone.

By the way, this "handoff" feature is available in other apps too and not just for phone calls. It's ideal for when you want to transfer what you're doing to another compatible and nearby iOS device (iPhone, iPad, or iPod touch) or Mac computer. It's part of Apple's Continuity feature over Wi-Fi and includes such apps as Calendar, Reminders, Messages, Mail, Contacts, Maps, and more.

Handoff should already be enabled on your Apple Watch, but if it isn't for whatever reason, Figure 5-7 shows the Apple Watch app on your iPhone and where in the Settings you can enable the feature: My Watch ➪ Settings ➪ General. Simply flick the tab to green to enable Handoff.

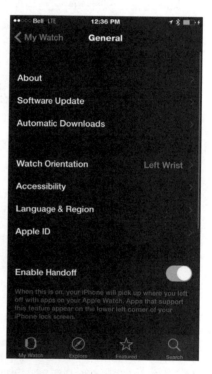

If an Apple Watch app can be "handed off" to iPhone, you should see the Handoff option inside the watch app, and once selected, you can simply tap the icon in the lower-left corner of the iPhone screen to complete the handoff to your phone.

Apple says this about a handoff: "When this is on, your iPhone will pick up where you left off with apps on your Apple Watch. Apps that support this feature appear on the lower left corner of your iPhone lock screen."

To use Bluetooth for handing off a call, when a call comes in, slide up from the bottom of the watch screen for a list of options, including handing a call off to another Bluetooth-enabled device — be it the iPhone itself, a hands-free Bluetooth headset, or perhaps a Bluetooth-enabled stereo in your vehicle. Doing this transfers the call to the desired device.

Figure 5-7: You can tweak a number of options in the Apple Watch app on your iPhone, including the ability to transfer activities to other Apple products. And you should also see an alert on your Apple Watch screen.

Also, don't forget about the Digital Touch feature built into Apple Watch. In supported apps, simply press and hold the screen to bring up a submenu of options. For example, when you're in the Phone app, as shown in Figure 5-8, you'll see options to access your Favorites (pulled from your iPhone):

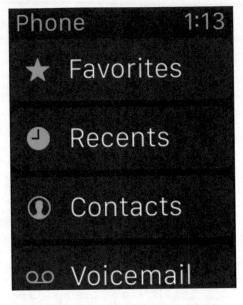

- ✔ **Recents:** Recent people you've spoken to.
- ✔ **Contacts:** Those from your iPhone.
- ✔ **Voicemail:** To quickly pick up your messages.

Figure 5-8: Press and hold the Apple Watch screen when inside the Phone app to bring up these handy shortcuts.

Receiving and Sending Messages

Many millions of iPhone users send messages from one iPhone to another device — whether it's a standard text (SMS) message or through Apple's own iMessage service. That might be a bit confusing because the app itself is called *Messages*, but iMessage is part of it, along with regular texting. The main advantage to iMessage over texting is it's free for you and anyone writing over Wi-Fi — and it's unlimited, so you can type and upload media as much as you want.

Apple Watch also houses a Messages app — supporting iMessage and text messages — although unlike the iPhone, you don't have a keyboard for you to type words on the watch.

But although you can't type on Apple Watch, you can send messages through voice dictation (or send the audio clip instead), tap on preset responses based on the context of messages you've received, or send animated emojis (cute and customizable icons) or your location on a map.

Receiving and responding to messages

You can keep you iPhone tucked away yet still correspond with important people in your life. When a message comes in (via iMessage or a text message), your Apple Watch vibrates on your wrist (and dings) to let you know you have a new message waiting to be read. (You can disable tactile feedback and sound in the Settings area of the Apple Watch app on your iPhone, as discussed in Chapter 11.)

Acknowledging a message

To receive, reply, and initiate a message to someone via your Apple Watch, follow these steps:

1. **If you feel a pulse and hear a tone, raise your wrist to see the message.**

   As shown in Figure 5-9, you should see a screen with whom the message is from, what he or she wrote, and perhaps an integrated image. You can scroll up and down by twisting the Digital Crown button if the message is longer than what's on the screen.

2. **To dismiss the message, lower your wrist or tap Dismiss at the bottom of the message.**

   Do this if you don't want to reply — or at least not right now. You can just exit the Messages app and return later.

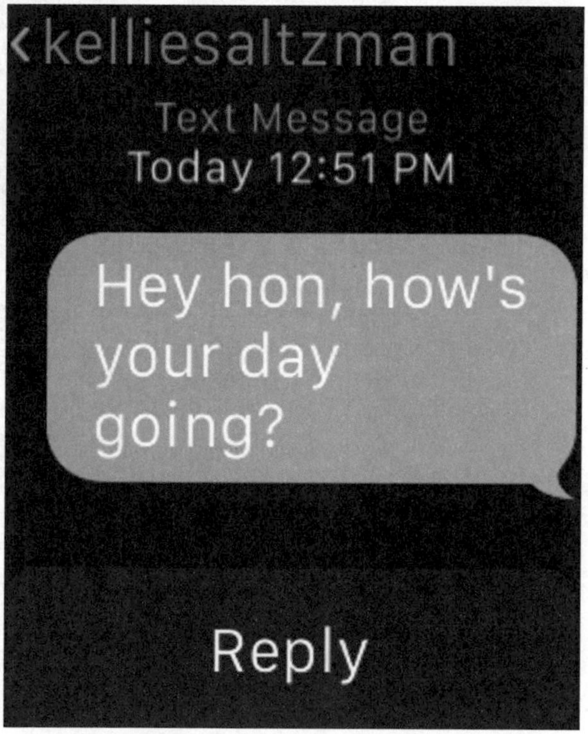

3. **If you want to reply to the message, tap Reply at the bottom of the screen and you should see multiple options.**

> ❮kelliesaltzman
> Text Message
> Today 12:51 PM
>
> Hey hon, how's your day going?
>
> Reply

Figure 5-9: An incoming message on Apple Watch.

Apple Watch suggests some preset words to reply with based on the context of the conversation, along with some preset responses you can choose from (such as Not Sure, Can't Talk Now, Talk later?). Twist the Digital Crown button to see all the responses and then tap one you like. To create a custom response in the Apple Watch app on your iPhone, see Chapter 11.

Replying to a message

If you want to reply to a message with your voice, follow these steps in the Messages app:

1. **Tap the microphone icon — as shown in Figure 5-10 — to speak (dictate) your reply and have it transcribed into text or sent as an audio clip.**

   Speak clearly into your wrist and you should see the words typed out as you say them.

2. **Tap Done in the top right of the screen and then select Send As Audio or Send As Text.**

   You should see a preview of the words before you send them. You can't change it if something isn't correct, so you have to tap Cancel in the top right and then say it again (perhaps slower and clearer).

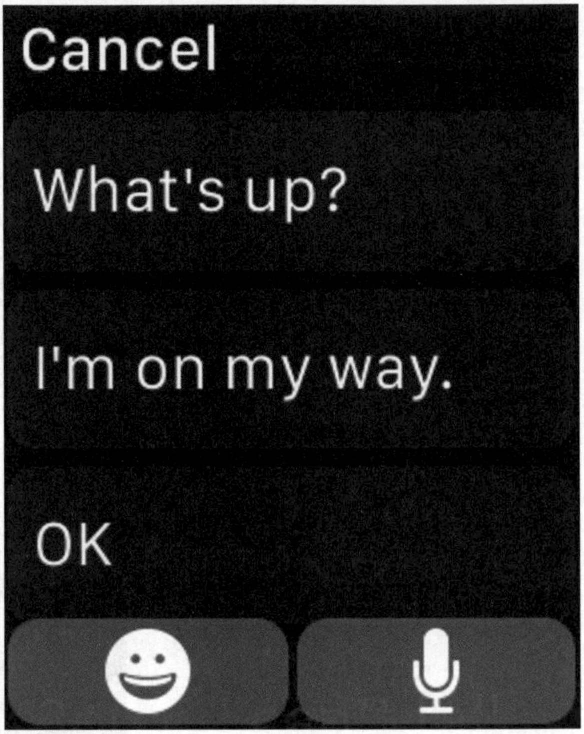

Figure 5-10: You must dictate your messages because Apple Watch doesn't have a keyboard.

Responding with animated emojis

To reply to a message with an emoji, follow these steps:

1. **Instead of replying with a preset message, tap the smiley face in the bottom left of the Apple Watch screen to launch the emoji selection list, as shown in Figure 5-11.**

   This brings up a number of emojis to choose from to express yourself in a more playful way.

2. **Twist the Digital Crown button to select the right emoji that conveys your message or feelings — whether it's a smile, a silly tongue hanging out, a sad face, a heart, or something else. Figure 5-12 shows some examples of emoji you can send.**

The small green bar in the top right of the screen shows you where your list of options starts and ends. Leave the emoji on the screen for a moment to see how it'll animate once received by someone else.

3. **When you find an emoji that fits the bill — maybe an animated thumbs-up or thumbs-down — tap Send in the top right of the screen to send it to the recipient.**

   If you decide against sending the emoji, tap Cancel in the top-left corner of the watch screen.

Figure 5-11: Tap the emoji icon to send a playful smiley face or another emoji instead of (or in addition to) your words.

Along with the animated emojis that fill up much of the Apple Watch screen, you can also send more traditional (static) emojis, as shown in Figure 5-13.

Figure 5-12: You have many emojis to choose from by spinning the Digital Crown.

Sending a message

You can send a new message through your Apple Watch in three ways — all of which require a nearby iPhone: from the Messages app, from your Friends ring, or by using Siri.

To send a message from your Apple Watch by using the Messages app, follow these steps:

1. **Press the Digital Crown button to go to the Home screen**

2. **Tap the Messages app.**

   This launches the Messages app, where you can read previously sent or received messages.

Figure 5-13: Select regular emoji if you don't want to send one of the fancier animated ones.

3. **To send a new message, press and hold the screen until the words New Message pop up — as shown in Figure 5-14 — and then tap them.**

   Alternatively, you can tap the Side button to open your Friends ring, press and hold the screen over someone's name or face (Digital Touch), and then select whether you'd like to call or message them, as also shown in Figure 5-14.

   Now you're ready to start a new message to someone.

4. **Tap Add Contact to select to whom to send the message.**

5. **Tap Create Message, which lets you dictate your message, as also shown in Figure 5-14.**

   Again, you have an option for Apple Watch to transcribe your words into text or you can send your message as a voice clip.

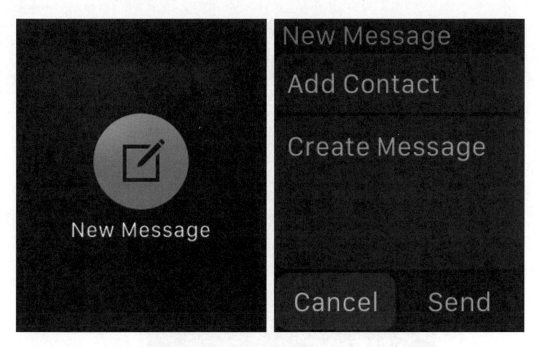

Figure 5-14: Once you tap New Message and choose a contact to whom to send a message, you can then tap Create Message to compose a message.

To send a message from your Apple Watch by using your Friends ring, follow these steps:

1. **Press the Side button to bring up your Friends ring.**

2. **Twist the Digital Crown button to find someone to message.**

   You don't need to press the Digital Crown button. You tap the person's initials or photo seen in the center of the watch — and just wait a second.

3. **Tap the Message icon — the speech bubble icon in the lower right of the watch screen.**

   This launches the Messages app. But remember, you can only add up to 12 people to your Friends ring through the Apple Watch app on iPhone, as discussed earlier in this chapter in the "Using the Friends Ring" section.

To send a message on your Apple Watch by using Siri, follow these steps:

1. **Lift your wrist and say "Hey, Siri" into your watch, followed by "Message ____ (person's name or number)." Figure 5-15 shows a request example.**

   You can also press and hold the Digital Crown button to activate Siri.

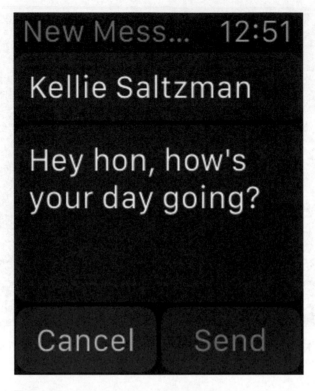

Figure 5-15: Impress your friends by sending a message effortlessly — all by using your voice.

2. **The Messages app opens up, and you should see the person to whom you want to send a message.**

   Dictate your message by tapping the microphone icon.

3. **Tap Send when you're done recording your message.**

   The person you're messaging with will momentarily receive the text or audio clip.

A superfast way to send a message to someone through Apple Watch is to raise your wrist and say "Hey, Siri, message _____ (person's name)" and then say "_____ (message)." Siri shows you the message before you send it. See Chapter 7 for more ways to use Siri to help you perform tasks with your Apple Watch.

You can also start a message on Apple Watch and continue it on your iPhone. As you can with calls and emails, it's easy to transfer messages to your iPhone, where you can pick up right where you left off. Apple Watch is meant for quick interactions, not lengthy ones. See the "Handing Off a Call to Your iPhone or via Bluetooth" section to learn more about handing off calls to your iPhone from your Apple Watch.

Receiving and Managing Emails on Apple Watch

Apple Watch would be a half-baked product if it could only be used for reading messages and not email. Thankfully, it can also deliver a decent mail experience on your wrist. I say "decent" because one thing you *can't* do on Apple Watch is send a new email or reply to an existing one. You can read and manage your mail, sure, but to reply, you have to open an email on your iPhone to type a response.

Apple Watch's inbox is synced with your iPhone, so you can browse by date, sender name, titles, contents, and attachment/VIP status or by the default All Inboxes, as shown in Figure 5-16. This is especially important for those who rely on email communication for work.

Along with reading an email, you can flag it, mark it as read or unread, or move it to the Trash.

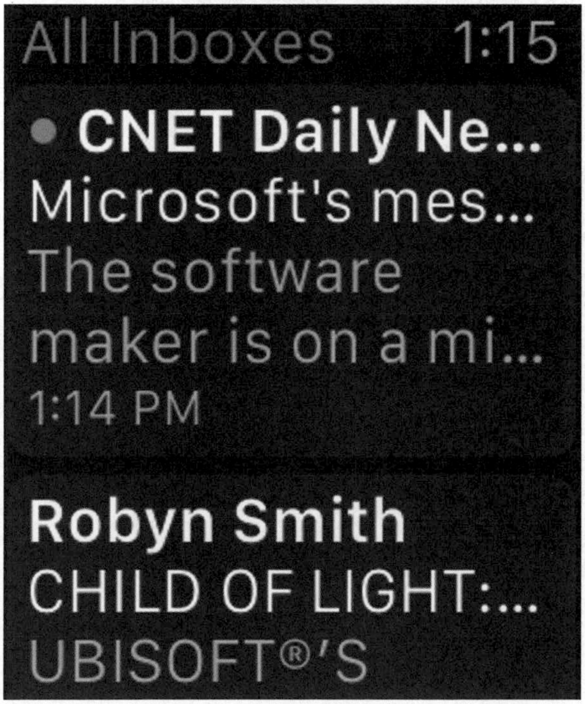

Figure 5-16: You can manage your inbox from your wrist.

To read and act on an email message, follow these steps:

1. **Press the Digital Crown button to go to the Home screen.**

2. **Tap the Mail app.**

   Or raise your wrist and say "Hey, Siri, Mail." Either action launches the Mail app and takes you right to your inbox.

3. **Use the Digital Crown button or your fingertip to scroll up and down through your emails — as shown in Figure 5-17 — and then tap the subject line to open one.**

   The email you selected fills up your Apple Watch screen and the others in your inbox won't be seen.

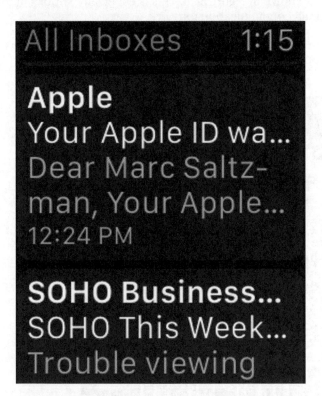

Figure 5-17: Use the Digital Crown button or your fingertip to scroll up and down through your inbox and then tap a message to select it.

4. **When in an email, press and hold on the screen until some options, such as Flag, Unread/Read, and Trash, appear, as shown in Figure 5-18.**

   If the email has already been read, you should see an option to mark it as Unread (to have it highlighted again).

It's important to understand you can't reply to an email on Apple Watch. You can read and manage your messages, but no options exist to dictate a response, like you can with other Apple Watch apps (such as Messages, Twitter, and Notes). Sad — but true.

Sending Taps, Sketches, and Heartbeats via Apple Watch

Just like with your iPhone, Apple Watch lets you communicate via phone and text, but it can also do some things your smartphone can't do. Collectively, these actions fall under the Digital Touch features — available exclusively to Apple Watch.

Call it wrist-to-wrist communication.

Digital Touch allows Apple Watch wearers to connect with other Apple Watch wearers in fun, unique, and sponta-neous ways. Specifically, Digital Touch offers three categories, as shown in Figure 5-19:

✔ **Sketch:** Draw something with your finger and the person you're send-ing it to sees it ani-mate on his or her Apple Watch.

Figure 5-18: Press and hold the Apple Watch screen to bring up a few options for dealing with email.

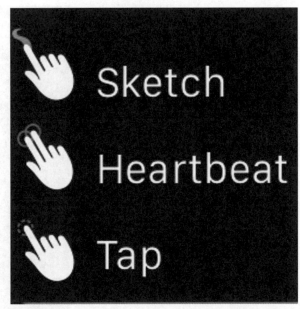

Figure 5-19: When you bring up your Friends ring on your Apple Watch, you can choose to send someone a special feature.

> ✔ **Tap:** Send gentle (and even customizable) taps to someone to let that person know you're thinking about him or her.
>
> ✔ **Heartbeat:** Your built-in heart rate monitor information is captured and sent to someone special so that person can feel it on his or her wrist.

Sketch

You can draw on your Apple Watch screen and the share your creation — a sketch — with another Apple Watch owner.

To create and send a sketch from your Apple Watch, follow these steps:

1. **Press the Side button to bring up your Friends ring — regardless of what you're doing on your Apple Watch.**

2. **Twist the Digital Crown button to select someone (or touch the person's initials on the screen to jump right there).**

   After selecting someone, you should see ways to reach out to that person at the bottom of the screen. If that person has an Apple Watch, you should see a Digital Touch icon, which looks like a hand with a forefinger extended.

3. **Tap the Digital Touch icon.**

   You can now draw, tap, or put two fingers on the screen to send your heartbeat.

   For sketches, start drawing on the black screen and you should see your image appear. You can draw a smiley face, a star, a heart, a flower, a sun, a fish, written-out words, or anything else you can think of. See Figure 5-20 for an example. Because your friend is wearing an Apple Watch, that person sees the drawing appear on his or her wrist just as you drew it. He or she knows it's from

Figure 5-20: This is a (poorly drawn!) example of what you can sketch and send to a friend's Apple Watch.

you because your name is in the top-left corner (which is the same for a tap and a heartbeat).

When sending a sketch, you can tap the small circle at the top right of the Apple Watch screen to change colors. See Figure 5-21 for a look at the seven colors offered in the palette.

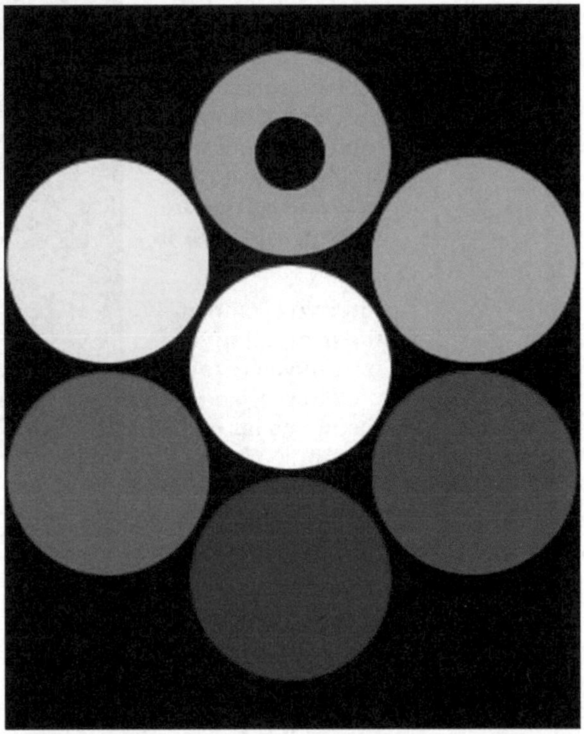

Apple Watch is little more than two square inches; therefore, don't expect to paint a masterpiece, but sketches are fun and creative ways to reach out to others. The person who receives a sketch can reply with one too, and you can chat back and forth like this to your heart's content.

Tap

Another unique way to use Digital Touch on Apple Watch is to send a tap to someone. As with the other Digital Touch features, that person needs to have an Apple Watch too. A tap is similar to a tactile version of a Facebook "poke" — a kind of "Hey, I've been thinking about you" type of notification.

Figure 5-21: You're not limited to just one color for a sketch. Tap the small circle, select another color, and then draw away.

To send a tap from your Apple Watch, follow these steps:

1. **Press the Side button to bring up your Friends ring — regardless of what you're doing on your Apple Watch.**

2. **Twist the Digital Crown button to select someone in your Friends ring or you can touch the person's initials on the screen to jump to that contact.**

   After selecting someone, you should see ways to reach out to that person at the bottom of the screen. If that person has an Apple Watch, you should see a Digital Touch icon, which looks like a hand with a forefinger extended.

You can now draw, tap, or put two fingers on the screen to send your heartbeat.

3. **To send a tap, use your fingers to tap a pattern on the screen, such as two quick taps in the top-left corner and a single press on the bottom right of the screen, as shown in Figure 5-22.**

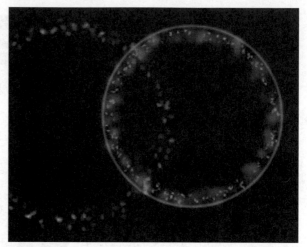

After you complete those taps, the person you're tapping to sees and feels the tap on his or her Apple Watch — visually presented as small and large rings that disappear — and he or she knows it's from you because your name is in the top-left corner (which is the same for a sketch and a heartbeat).

Figure 5-22: Send a custom tap to someone else with an Apple Watch and that person should see and feel it on his or her wrist.

The recipient can "play" the pattern again by tapping in the upper-right corner. If and when the person you're tapping with replies with a Digital Touch, he or she can choose to reply with something else, such as a sketch or a heartbeat instead of another tap.

Heartbeat

Sending your heartbeat is another way to reach out and flirt with someone — from your Apple Watch to another person's Apple Watch. Is that romantic or what?!

To send a heartbeat from your Apple Watch, follow these steps:

1. **Press the Side button to bring up your Friends ring — regardless of what you're doing on your Apple Watch.**

   You should see up to 12 contacts you can reach out to.

2. **Twist the Digital Crown button to select someone — whether you choose to go clockwise or counterclockwise. Or just tap someone to go immediately to that contact (but just wait a moment for it to launch that person full screen).**

3. **Tap the Digital Touch icon, which has a hand with a forefinger extended.**

   After selecting someone, you should see ways to reach out to that person at the bottom of the screen. If that person has an Apple Watch, you should see a Digital Touch icon, which looks like a hand with a forefinger extended.

   You can now draw, tap, or put two fingers on the screen to send your heartbeat.

4. **Press two fingers on the screen at the same time and then Apple Watch's heart rate monitor (which is underneath the watch) immediately starts calculating your heart rate.**

   After a few seconds, your heartbeat — as shown in Figure 5-23 — is sent to (and felt by) your significant other or friend. He or she knows it's from you because your name is in the top-left corner (which is the same for a sketch and a tap).

   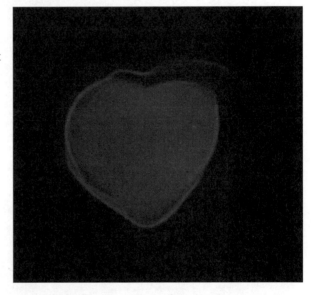

   Figure 5-23: Send your heartbeat to a friend's or your better half's Apple Watch, which is seen here as a beating heart. You just need two fingers to do so.

   Okay, this might sound a little gimmicky, but it might just brighten up your friend's or loved one's day if he or she is having a rotten one. Just don't send it to the wrong person, such as your boss or your best friend's spouse — in case someone gets the wrong idea.

6

In the Know: Staying Informed With Apple Watch

*W*hen people ask me "Why do I need a smartwatch?" I usually answer with something like "convenience." A wearable device on your wrist is ideal for quick bits of information — when and where you need it. Rather than pulling out your smartphone or your tablet, you can simply glance down with your eyes to get what you need while on the go.

This chapter focuses mostly on how Apple Watch shows you information that's relevant to you. For example, you can access weather information for today or for the next week. Or even in another city. Or multiple cities. Do you like playing the market or want to see how your own public company is doing? Select which company's stock price and performance are important in your world — all updated in real time.

I also describe how to add this information to your watch face as one of the complications options. I also cover how to access Glances and Notifications on Apple Watch for a number of installed apps. I round it all off with using Apple Watch for calendar alerts and accessing maps on your wrist.

Accessing Real-Time Weather and Stock Information and Much More

Apple Watch comes with many built-in Apple Watch apps (see Table 1-1 in Chapter 1 for a list of them) — and Weather and Stocks are two of them.

Sure, you can choose not to see this information on your smartwatch if you're not interested in one or both of these — simply unselect either or both of them in the Apple Watch app on your iPhone, as covered in Chapter 11 — but this information should be timely and interesting for many (hence, Apple adding them in without your having to download specific apps).

Checking the weather

The Weather app displays your current location's temperature and a graphical representation of expected precipitation and conditions over much of the day (by the hour) as well as a week-ahead view — and for multiple locations if desired.

To use the Weather app on your Apple Watch, follow these steps:

1. **Press the Digital Crown button to go to the Home screen.**

2. **Tap the Weather app.**

   Once the app launches, you should see the temperature and weather for your current location, as shown in Figure 6-1. The temperature is in the center of the app, surrounded by a 12-hour look at the day and an associated icon, such as a sun, a cloud, a rain-cloud, snowflakes, and so on. If you

Figure 6-1: Whether it's a local city or faraway cities, get real-time weather conditions from the Weather app.

live in the United States, the temperature is displayed in Fahrenheit (a choice you make when setting up the watch); it's displayed in Celsius in Canada and other countries that use the metric system or if you make that choice yourself. The name of the city is in the top left of the screen and the current time is in the top right.

3. **Swipe down with your fingertip or twist the Digital Crown button toward you to scroll down the app. This shows you a ten-day forecast, as shown in Figure 6-2. Or press the screen (Digital Touch) for more information.**

Figure 6-2: The more you scroll down, the more weather information you can see. Or press the screen firmly and select additional information.

The further down you swipe or twist the Digital Crown button, the further ahead in the week you can go. You can see each day's high and low temperatures and predicted precipitation — all courtesy of the Weather Channel. Scroll back up to the top of the Weather app by twisting the Digital Crown button away from you or use your fingertip to swipe up.

4. **To see other cities you've selected to keep track of, swipe to the right or left to pull up the weather there, as shown in Figure 6-3. You can change the cities you follow in the Apple Watch app on iPhone; see Chapter 11 for more on doing this.**

Small white dots at the bottom of the app's screen show you how many pages (cities) you've selected. You can add or remove cities in the Apple Watch app on the iPhone. Open the app and select My Watch, followed by Settings and then Weather.

Figure 6-3: Flick to the left or right to access weather information in other cities. Customize what you see by using the Apple Watch app on iPhone.

Don't forget you can use Siri to call up weather information. Simply say "Hey, Siri" or press and hold the Digital Crown button, followed by a question, such as "What's it like outside?" or "Do I need a raincoat?" Or give a command, such as "Tell me the weather." Actually, you can just say "Weather." If you don't specify a location — like the examples provided here — Siri assumes you want to know your local information. See Chapter 7 for more on using Siri to help you perform tasks with your Apple Watch.

Following the stock market

To keep an eye on the stock market, Apple Watch offers you a quick glance at any public company's stock price and performance for when (and where) you'd like it. It's similar to the Stocks app on iPhone — but tailored to the smaller Apple Watch screen. The process is similar to looking at the weather — and it's just as customizable.

To use the Stocks apps on your Apple Watch, follow these steps:

1. **Press the Digital Crown button to go to the Home screen.**

2. **Tap the Stocks app.**

   If you didn't tweak what stocks you'd like to see — by going into the Stocks area of the Apple Watch app on iPhone; see Chapter 11 for more on doing this — you should see the current value of major stock indices, such as the Dow Jones Industrial Average, as well as such companies as Apple and Starbucks, as shown in Figure 6-4.

   Each company you follow on the stock market is listed by its traded name (such as AAPL for Apple), the current stock price underneath the name (such as $126.41), and whether the stock is up (in green) or down (in red) and by how much, such as a green +1.15.

Stocks	1:39
^GSPTSE	-0.54%
15,264.39	
DOW J	-0.57%
17,931.90	
AAPL	-2.29%
125.70	
SBUX	-1.24%
50.02	

Figure 6-4: See all kinds of stock price and performance information on any publicly traded company.

3. **You can learn more information about each company or exchange by tapping its name. Figure 6-5 shows an example.**

   This includes the full company name, point and percentage changes, and market cap.

   You can have a number of companies listed — all organized within the Apple Watch app on iPhone. See Chapter 11 for more on third-party apps.

4. **After you've selected a company or exchange, swipe down on the Stocks app on Apple Watch to show even more information, such as a graph view that lets you track its performance over the past day, week, month, or six months, as shown in Figure 6-6.**

<^DJI   1:39

Dow Jones
Industrial Average

17,928.40

-107.13 (-0.59%)

LOW | HIGH

17,894.43 | 18,033.33

Figure 6-5: Despite its small screen, Apple Watch can give you a ton of information about the stock market, such as this snapshot of the Dow Jones Industrial Average.

Swipe to the right at any time to go back to the main Stocks app screen with multiple indices and companies listed. You can also ask Siri to tell you the stock price of a given company or the performance of a stock index. You can access Siri by saying "Hey, Siri," followed by your question or command, or press the Digital Crown button in any app you're in to ask Siri about a particular company.

Figure 6-6: Swipe down in the Stocks app for additional information for an exchange, as shown here, or for a publicly traded company.

Adding Weather and Stocks to Your Watch Face Screen

Apple Watch lets you customize your watch face in a variety of different ways — see Chapter 4 for more on doing that — including the option to add complications.

To refresh your memory, complications are extra information you want visible on the watch face itself — such as weather and stocks — so you can see it when you're checking the time. Depending on which watch face you choose, complications are usually reserved for the four corners of the screen and perhaps the bottom center. When you tap on the piece of information provided, such as the weather, it opens up the corresponding app for a deeper look.

To add weather and stock information — or other complications, such as moon phase, sunrise and sunset information, alarm clocks, timers, and so on — to your watch face, follow these steps:

1. **Press and hold the screen when viewing a watch face.**

   This enables Force Touch and launches the Faces gallery.

2. **Swipe left or right to select a clock face you like.**

3. **Tap Customize near the bottom of the screen to add more information to each watch screen.**

   You can adjust the color of the hands and add or remove details, such as the second hand, by twisting the Digital Crown button.

4. **Swipe to the left to go to the last customization screen, which takes you to complications, as shown in Figure 6-7.**

   This is where you can add weather and stock quotes to the watch face you've selected.

5. **Tap the areas you want to customize (seen in green in Figure 6-7) and then twist the Digital Crown button to select what you'd like.**

   Repeat the process by tapping the other areas of the face you want to change. Remember, you won't have the same options for all watch faces. The watch face in Figure 6-7 doesn't allow for stock information, for example, but other watch faces do.

Figure 6-7: Add weather, stock information, and more to the preinstalled watch faces. Information varies by the watch face you choose, but this one allows for weather in the lower-left corner.

6. **Press the Digital Crown button when you're done customizing.**

7. **After you make your choices, press the Digital Crown button again to go back to the Home screen.**

   After you've set your watch face, don't forget you can tap on each of the complications, such as weather or stock quotes, to go directly to the relevant app. See Chapter 4 for more on complications.

You can take a screenshot of whatever you're doing on Apple Watch. Simply press the Digital Crown button and the Side button at the same time and you should see the screen briefly flash white. Now check your iPhone's Photos app. Your newly captured image should be there.

Using Glances on Apple Watch

Because Apple Watch is meant to give you a quick look at information that's relevant to you, you might consider Glances to be a kind of summary screen for many of your apps. You can choose which apps you want Glances for — selected in the Settings area of the Apple Watch app on an iPhone; see Chapter 11 for more on changing settings — but many of the built-in apps support Glances, such as Weather, Stocks, Messages, Mail, Calendar, Activity, Workout, Passbook, Music, and World Clock.

You can use fingertip gestures on the watch's screen to access your Glances. Chances are, you'll use Glances quite often, so knowing how to use them will come in handy.

To use Glances on your Apple Watch, follow these steps:

1. **Swipe up from the bottom of the watch screen to open Glances.**

   This bite-sized information is full screen on your watch face, but you can't scroll down for more information. To go to the app itself, tap the screen, which opens the app related to the information.

2. **Swipe left or right to scroll through all your Glances.**

   You can cycle through every app that has Glances, as shown in Figure 6-8.

   Many third-party apps for Apple Watch also support Glances, including social media apps (such as Facebook and Twitter); finance tools (such as Mint); sports apps (such as ESPN); airlines (such as United); news organizations (such as the *Wall Street Journal* and *USA Today*); productivity tools (such as Evernote); and so on.

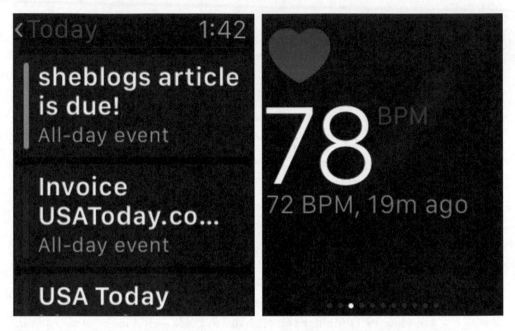

Figure 6-8: Glances are available for most preinstalled apps, such as Calendar and Activity (seen here).

Mastering Notifications on Apple Watch

Just as you swipe up from the watch face screen for Glances, you can swipe down for Notifications. Or they can just appear on your wrist in a timely fashion if you prefer.

As covered in Chapter 11, you can select which apps can give you Notifications on Apple Watch, as shown in Figure 6-9.

Notifications pull information from your iPhone, such as if someone liked your photo on Instagram, if your favorite game wants you to know someone is attacking your virtual kingdom, or if the New York Yankees won the doubleheader. Likewise, a news outlet, such as *USA Today*, might let you know the president is about to give a speech or if weather is taking a turn for the worse in your area. See Figure 6-10 for a look at a Notification tied to the USA Today app.

You should receive a gentle *tap* on your wrist to tell you about the news based on the apps you choose to give you Notifications.

TIP

If you're not feeling the Notifications on your wrist, you can dial up extra vibration by selecting Prominent Haptic within the Apple Watch's Sound and Haptics settings area. Now those buzzes on your wrist will feel more pronounced. You can enable Prominent Haptic in the Settings app on Apple Watch.

Just like on your iPhone or iPad, swipe down from the top of the Apple Watch Home screen to access your Notification Center. Here, you can scroll up or down with your finger or you can twist the Digital Crown button to see your next calendar appointment, how your stocks are doing, and perhaps a look at traffic on the way to the office.

To use Notifications on your Apple Watch, follow these steps:

1. **From the watch face screen, swipe down from the top of the screen to open the Notification Center.**

   Remember to start swiping down from the very top of the watch case — on the rim — to successfully pull up the information you want. Swiping from the middle of the screen doesn't work.

2. **Use your fingertip to swipe up and down for additional information or twist the Digital Crown button.**

   To go back to your Home screen, press the Digital Crown button.

Just as many preinstalled Apple Watch apps support Notifications and are on by default, many third-party apps do too. It's up to the app developer to add a Notification feature to the app. As shown in Chapter 11, you can enable or disable

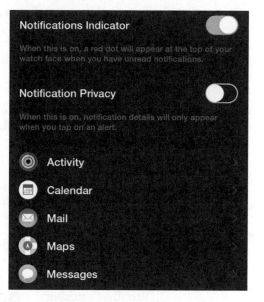

Figure 6-9: In the Apple Watch app on iPhone, you can select which Notifications you'd like on your Apple Watch. In each of the apps installed on your watch — a few are seen here — tap the app and then flick the tab to green to receive Notifications.

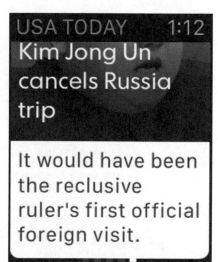

Figure 6-10: You can swipe down from the watch face screen to access your Notifications, including from third-party apps.

individual app Notifications in the Settings area of the Apple Watch app on your iPhone.

Accessing Your Calendar on Apple Watch

Because your Apple Watch is wirelessly tethered to your smartphone, you can access handy calendar information on your wrist. In fact, the Calendar app not only syncs with your iPhone, but it also syncs with iCloud if you use Apple's popular cloud service to store and access information.

Featuring day, week, and month views — including support for reminders, invitations, Glances, and Notifications — the Calendar app on Apple Watch shows you a list of upcoming events.

To use the Calendar app on your Apple Watch, follow these steps:

1. **Press the Digital Crown button to go to the Home screen.**

2. **Tap the Calendar app.**

   This launches the Calendar app. By default, you should see the current Today view — with your upcoming events listed in chronological order.

3. **Use your fingertip to scroll down to see future dates or twist the Digital Crown button toward you.**

   Figure 6-11 shows an example of an upcoming event.

   This experience is similar to the Calendar app on iPhone. The current time is also listed in the top right of the Calendar app.

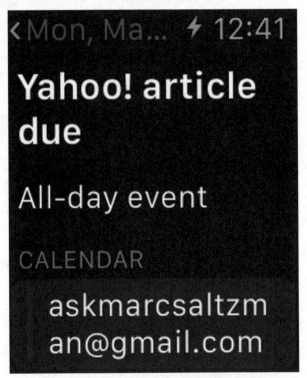

Figure 6-11: The Calendar app offers a look ahead — beyond that day — if you want to preview your upcoming week.

4. In the main Calendar app screen, tap the Today tab in the top left to access the Week or Month view. If you want to look at a date (such as Friday, October 16), just tap the day on the calendar for a Day view.

See Figure 6-12 for a look at the Month view.

In Month view, you can swipe left or right to move forward or backward through time or twist the Digital Crown button if you prefer.

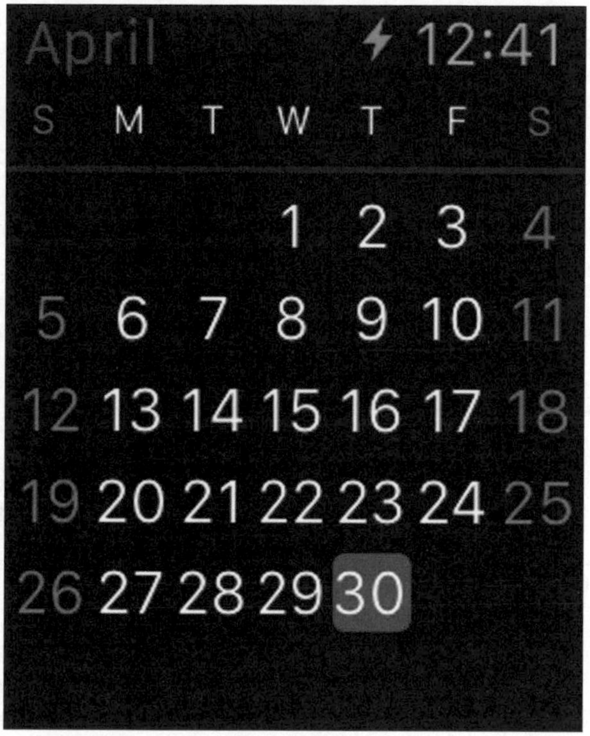

Just like you can set Reminders on your iPhone, iPad, or iPod touch, you can activate Siri on your Apple Watch and say something like "At 6 p.m., remind me to call Mom." It doesn't make a Calendar entry for this event, but you're reminded with a sound, a vibration on your wrist, and a text. Remember, Apple Watch has no keyboard, so you must dictate the reminder. See Chapter 7 for more ways to use Siri to help you accomplish tasks with Apple Watch.

Figure 6-12: See what's happening a month at a time and then tap a day for a chronological view of what events you have on a given day.

5. To add a new event, press and hold the Apple Watch screen while inside the Calendar app.

You're prompted to tap New and then select a date and time for the event. You'll also speak into your wrist for the title of your event. You can speak loudly, as Apple's dictation is quite good, but try to talk clearly and with as little ambient noise around you as possible.

Don't forget, Apple Watch pulls calendar events from your iPhone. And you don't always have to manually check your calendar for upcoming appointments because you should receive a Notification about it (and feel a slight pulse). Some users like to be reminded an hour before an event, for example, while others might only want a five-minute reminder. This is all handled in your iPhone's Calendar app.

Also, when you receive calendar invitations, you can accept or decline immediately and even email the organizer using preset responses.

To accept or decline a Calendar invitation or to reply to the organizer from your Apple Watch, following these steps:

1. **If someone sends you a calendar invite via email or message, you should receive a Notification with the proposed meeting date, time, and information, such as "Natalie's B-Day Party, September 19, 2015, 6 p.m."**

   This is where you have a chance to act on it — and you won't have to reach for your iPhone.

2. **Use your finger to swipe down on the Notification or twist the Digital Crown button and then you can tap Accept, Maybe, or Decline.**

   You can't suggest an alternative date or time or anything — like you can do with some email programs — but this lets the organizer receive some sort of response.

3. **Swipe up to respond to an invitation, firmly press (Digital Touch) the display while you're looking at the event details, and then choose to call the organizer or send a voice message recording.**

   You can also perform all these functions inside the Calendar app — instead of via a Notification — by tapping on the meeting details and choosing to accept, decline, or reply.

Don't forget that you can raise your wrist and say "Hey, Siri" or press and hold the Digital Crown button and then say something like "Add calendar entry, dentist appointment, for 9 a.m. tomorrow." This spoken text is added to your calendar and synced with your iPhone too.

Or use Siri to ask Apple Watch about upcoming events, such as "What's on my calendar today?" "What's next on my calendar?" or "When is my appointment at the dentist?" See Chapter 7 for more ways to use Siri to help you complete tasks with your Apple Watch.

You don't need your iPhone to receive calendar alerts on your Apple Watch. Therefore, if you go on a run or accidentally leave your iPhone at the office, you can still see existing calendar entries, but you can't add one. Why? Because Apple Watch doesn't have a keyboard, you have to use Siri to dictate new appointments, which isn't possible without the iPhone.

Navigating the Maps App

Apple Maps — or simply Maps — is one of the built-in Apple Watch apps. It allows you to get directions from your current location to a destination of your choosing — with the app calculating the best route.

You should see — and feel — the turn-by-turn navigation instructions to guide you along the way, and you can always search for nearby businesses, such as a restaurant or a gas station, simply by asking Siri for it.

To use the Maps app on your Apple Watch, follow these steps:

1. **Press the Digital Crown button to go to the Home screen.**

2. **Tap Maps.**

   This launches the Maps app. An overhead map of your current location appears on the Apple Watch screen, and you can swipe in a given direction to move the map around or you can twist the Digital Crown button if you want to see nearby streets or businesses.

3. **Tap the blue icon in the lower left of the screen — as shown in Figure 6-13 — to return to your current location.**

   This recenters the map to your specific location. You can also zoom in and out by twisting the Digital Crown button.

4. **To find a location, press and hold the screen to activate Siri and then speak an address or business name.**

5. **Tap the blue word Done in the top right of the screen when you're finished.**

   The next time you do a search in Maps, you should also see

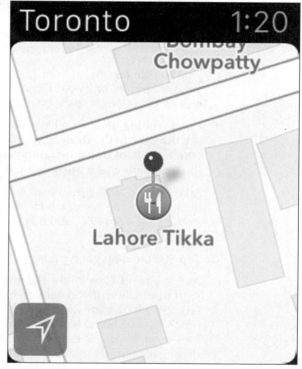

Figure 6-13: The Maps app offers a number of features to help you with directions or find local businesses.

your last searched addresses below the Dictation tab, as shown in Figure 6-14.

A firm press on the screen uses Apple Watch's Digital Touch feature. If the location is a business, you can tap it on the map to bring up information, such as the address and phone number (which you can call), hours of operation and if it's open at that exact moment, and its star rating (average user rating out of five stars — via Yelp). You should also see an estimate on how long it might take to get there by foot or by car. Figure 6-15 shows information about a restaurant and how long it might take to travel there.

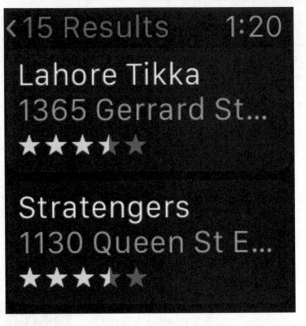

Figure 6-14: Ask and ye shall receive. You need to use your voice to get directions or find a local business.

6. **Upon landing on a searched destination in the Maps app, you should see the time to the desired location by car or by foot — so you can tap which mode of transportation you're using — and you should also see the destination as a pushpin on the map.**

Addresses in Messages, Email, Calendar, and other apps are highlighted in blue and underlined, which means they're tappable. Tap the address, such as 123 Yonge St., and it launches that address in the Maps app for you. Neat, huh?

7. **Tap Start to map your route.**

And you're off! Now follow the instructions as you make your way to your destination. If you need to turn right, a steady series of a dozen taps are felt on your wrist at the intersection you're approaching. To turn left, you should feel three pairs of two taps. Of course, you can also look down at your screen for visual cues (while on foot and not while driving of course!).

Figure 6-15: Get information on a local business — provided by Yelp — simply by tapping on its name. You can also read customer reviews as well as see how long it might take to get to your destination.

As you can with all other built-in apps, use Siri to access Maps information whenever you like. Either raise your wrist and say "Hey, Siri," followed by something like "Show me 5 Main Street in Beverly, Kansas" to see it on a map or "Hey, Siri, give me directions to the Golden Gate Bridge." You can also press the Digital Crown button to activate Siri. See Chapter 7 for more on using Siri to help you perform tasks with your Apple Watch.

Part III
It's All in the Wrist

In this part . . .

✔ Gain a helping hand from Siri, which can assist you in completing tasks with your Apple Watch, including tips and tricks to speed up your requests. And then have some fun by learning several humorous questions you can ask Siri.

✔ Get physical with help from the Activity and Workout apps on your Apple Watch, including setting and modifying goals, receiving real-time feedback on your performance, and earning rewards for your achievements.

✔ Store music, podcasts, audiobooks, and radio plays—with help from your iPhone—on your Apple Watch and take your favorite media with you anywhere. Then, learn how you can use your Apple Watch to control your Apple TV and your iTunes library.

✔ Turn your Apple Watch into a virtual wallet by setting up Apple Pay. Then, explore the Passbook app, where you can store movie and concert tickets, boarding passes, coupons, loyalty cards, and much more.

7

Siri Supersized: Gaining the Most From Your Personal Assistant

*W*hile most Apple Watch wearers will interact using their fingers on their wrist-mounted gadget — tapping, pressing, or swiping the screen or accessing the two buttons along the side — you can get more done in less time if you simply talk to your watch.

Already an iconic feature on other Apple products — such as iPhone, iPod touch, and iPad — Siri (pronounced "sear-ree") is your own voice-activated personal assistant. Using your words instead of your fingers to ask for information or give a command is a very natural, fast, and simple way to access content. Talking to your tech gadget is more intuitive than typing or tapping — and getting a humanlike response is more meaningful too — so Apple Watch wearers will no doubt benefit from the fact the watch has a built-in microphone and speaker.

As long as your watch is wirelessly tethered to your Internet-connected iPhone — required to send your words to Apple's servers for processing — Siri might just be the best feature of Apple Watch.

Of course, you might not always be in a place where you can talk openly (such as in a quiet boardroom meeting) or you might not have Internet access at that moment (such as on an airplane without Wi-Fi), but most of the time, you can use Siri to give you what you want — and quickly.

But you don't know where to start, you say? No problem.

Shameless plug alert: As the author of the book *Siri For Dummies*, I show you in this chapter all the different ways you can use Siri to get information on your Apple Watch.

Setting Up Siri on Your Apple Watch

Because Siri requires your iPhone, you don't need to do anything to set up Siri on Apple Watch.

This is because you've already set up Siri on your iPhone when you first turned on your device. As you may or may not recall, your iPhone asked you if you want Siri (and, yes, you can also enable or disable it in the Settings➪General➪Siri area of your iPhone) and what language you prefer. You have nearly 30 options, including English, French, Spanish, Italian, German, Chinese, Japanese, Korean, and Russian — to name a few.

Choosing a language and dialect isn't just so Siri can speak in a language you understand; it's also to let your new personal assistant better understand you. For example, someone from the United States or Canada will say "Call Mom" differently than an English-speaking person from the United Kingdom or Australia. One might sound more like "Coll mum" or "Cull mam" and so on. See Figure 7-1 for a look at the Siri options on iPhone.

In fact, you can choose from seven different kinds of English for Siri: Australia, Canada, India, New Zealand, Singapore, United Kingdom, and United States. Obviously, Americans have various accents too — differences definitely exist between speakers from Long Island, Boston, Dallas, and Minneapolis, for example — but American English can be vastly different from the English spoken in London or Sydney. Thus, be sure to choose the correct language from the list or you may have some difficulties understanding Siri — and vice versa.

It's also important to note Siri has a female voice in the United States by default, but you can change it to a male voice if you like. For this reason, I usually refer to Siri as "it" to keep language universal.

To make other changes to Siri, go to Settings➪General➪Siri on your iPhone. Some other choices you have in the Siri settings of iPhone include the following:

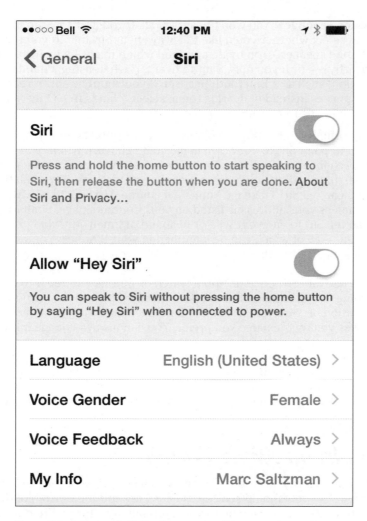

Figure 7-1: Select your Siri options on your iPhone, such as voice gender and language.

✔ **Allow "Hey, Siri":** One option you have when using Siri is whether you want to simply say "Hey, Siri" instead of pressing the Home button on an iPhone or pressing the Digital Crown button on Apple Watch. If you enable this feature in your iPhone's settings, you can simply raise your wrist to your mouth and say "Hey, Siri," followed by your question or command. For the hands-free "Hey, Siri" feature to work on an iPhone, your iPhone has to be connected to a power source, such as your car's 12V port (the cigarette lighter), but this isn't required to enable "Hey, Siri" on your Apple Watch. Just raise your wrist and speak.

✔ **Voice Feedback:** You won't hear Siri talk through the watch, but you can select whether you'd like to always hear Siri talk to you through the iPhone speaker — on by default (and which might be heard by those nearby) — or if you only want to hear Siri when using a hands-free option, such as a Bluetooth headset. If you simply want to read Siri's responses instead of hearing them, select "Hands-free Only" and don't use a hands-free product.

✔ **My Info:** Selecting this tab opens up your Contacts app. Why? It wants you to point Siri to your own name so it can learn where you live and those close to you. If you don't have an entry in your Contacts with your own information, you need to create one. Once you fill out all the fields, you can tell Siri "Take me home." Of course, Siri won't know where that is unless your address is listed on your Contacts page. Similarly, you can tell Siri to call your wife or husband or email your dad or text your mom — all of which can be identified in your iPhone's Contacts page (yes, fields exist there for people close to you).

You can activate Siri on your Apple Watch or iPhone and tell it to call you something else. Instead of Robert, you can say "Siri, call me Bob" for an abbreviation or "Siri, call me Junior" for a nickname. Going forward, Siri addresses you by the name you prefer. You can always change it if you like.

Unlike other speech-to-text technology, including those offered by other smartphones, Siri works on the *operating system* level and knows which app to open based on your request. Most other smartphones require you to first open an app *before* you tap the microphone to speak. You don't need to do this for Siri.

Talking to Siri on Apple Watch

When you ask Siri a question — such as "What's the weather like in Seattle tomorrow?" — you should see colors dance around the bottom of the watch screen to confirm it's listening to you. Stop talking after you're done and you should hear a beep to confirm Siri is now processing your request.

If you make a mistake while asking Siri a question (maybe you accidentally said the wrong person's name to text) or perhaps Siri didn't hear you clearly, you can tap the screen to nullify the request and then ask again. You should hear the familiar *ping* tone to confirm Siri is listening for your new request.

The final thing you should see is when Siri performs your desired action. Siri might open up a map, an email message, a calendar entry, or a restaurant listing or show you such information as the score of your favorite team's last game (without even opening an app). Unlike iPhone, however, Siri won't speak to you through Apple Watch — you should just see the information. For example, if it's a dictionary definition or a numerical equation you're after, you should see words like "Here you go" or "This might answer your question" and then Siri shows you the information on the screen.

Because all requests to Siri are uploaded to a server, it's not unheard of for the server to be temporarily inaccessible — but it doesn't happen very often. Siri will apologize to you and ask that you please try again later. A problem with Siri *isn't* an indication of a problem with your Apple Watch or iPhone, so don't fret. The outage is usually only a couple minutes (if that), but it's something you should be aware of.

To maximize Siri's performance on Apple Watch, follow these tips:

- **Keep your iPhone close:** You need to have your iPhone nearby to perform all tasks — even if it's a local task, such as asking Siri to jot down some words in a shopping list app (which doesn't seem like it needs the Internet). Whether it's a cellular signal you're using (make sure you see a few bars in the top left of your phone) or Wi-Fi (a wireless network), you need decent reception to get quick results from Siri. This is critical.

- **Speak clearly:** I know this can be difficult to be conscious of, but the less you mumble and the more you articulate your words, the better Siri works. Don't worry: Siri is remarkably keen on picking up what you say (and even what you mean), so you don't need to speak like a robot. Just be aware that you'll get better results with clearer speech.

- **Find a quiet place:** A lot of background noise isn't great for Siri because it might not be able to pick up what you're saying very well. The quieter the environment, the better Siri can understand your instructions. This might be tough if you're in a crowded restaurant, driving with the window open, or walking down a busy street, of course, so you might need to speak a little louder and closer to the Apple Watch microphone.

Using Siri Effectively on Apple Watch

Everything you can do with your fingers, you can do with Siri — if not more — and in less time. A good way to demonstrate its versatility is to look at a number of built-in Apple Watch apps and some examples of how you can use Siri to get what you want.

Remember, you don't need to open an app first to start talking to Siri — but you do need to enable Siri on Apple Watch when you first set up the watch, as shown in Figure 7-2. And you must also enable Siri to work hands-free in the Apple Watch's Settings tab. Enable "Hey, Siri" to lift your wrist and speak — without having to press the Digital Crown button.

It works in the main Home screen mode, while accessing the clock, or in any app you find yourself in, such as asking Siri for map directions even though you're using the Music app at the time.

If you're unsure about all the things Siri is capable of, say "Siri, what can you do?" on your iPhone and you should see a huge list of things!

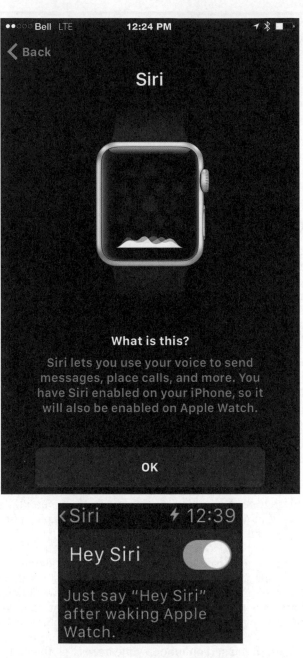

Figure 7-2: When you first set up Apple Watch via the iPhone app, you're prompted to enable Siri on your wrist. Then, on Apple Watch, open up the Settings apps and allow for "Hey, Siri" if you want to activate your personal assistant without pressing the Digital Crown button.

To activate Siri, raise your wrist and say "Hey, Siri," followed by your question or command. Alternatively, you can press and hold the Digital Crown button to activate Siri. With the latter option, you don't have to say "Siri" or "Hey, Siri" first (although all my friends seem to do that!).

Clock/World Clock apps

Some examples of using Siri for time-related tasks include:

- ✔ "What time is it?"
- ✔ "What time is it in Dubai?" See Figure 7-3 for what you might see after asking this.
- ✔ "What time will the sun rise in Brisbane?"
- ✔ "How many days until Christmas?"
- ✔ "What day of the week will it be on June 10, 2017?"

Messages app

Some examples of using Siri for sending and receiving messages include:

Figure 7-3: Ask all kinds of time-related questions and you'll get answers, such as the local time or, as pictured here, the time in another city.

- ✔ "Read me my messages."
- ✔ "Do I have any messages from ___ (name)?"
- ✔ "Text my wife 'Hey, hon, how's your day going?'"
- ✔ "Text 212-555-1212. 'I'm looking forward to our after-work drink tonight.'"
- ✔ "Text Julie and Frank 'Where are you guys?'"
- ✔ "Reply 'That's awesome news!'"

Something fun to try with Siri on Apple Watch — which may amuse the kids — is to ask Siri to remind you about something really far in the future. For example, I asked Siri to remind me to kiss my wife in 10,000 years, and I was asked if it should be placed in my calendar then. (I hope someone finds a cure for mortality soon!)

Phone/Contacts apps

Some examples of using Siri for making calls or looking up Contacts information include:

- "Call Mom."
- "Dial 212-555-1212."
- "What's Michael Smith's address?"
- "What's my sister's work address?"
- "Learn how to pronounce my name."
- "Show Jennifer's location."

Mail app

Some examples of using Siri for looking for email include:

- "Show me my email" or "Check email."
- "Do I have any email from Apple?" See Figure 7-4 to see what happens when you ask for email from a specific person or company.
- "Show the email from Natasha yesterday."

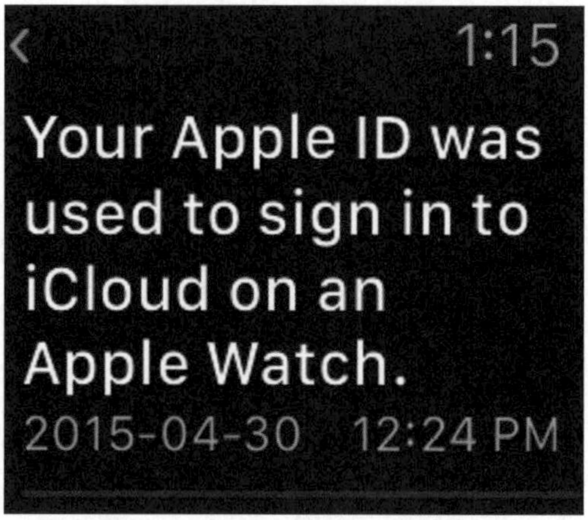

Calendar app

Some examples of using Siri for accessing Calendar information include:

Figure 7-4: Ask for mail from Apple and Siri will show it to you — whether you want to see what came in by time or by person/company.

- "Show me what appointments I have on Monday."
- "When is my next meeting?"
- "When's my next appointment?"
- "Move my 12 p.m. meeting to 1 p.m."
- "Cancel the meeting at 4 p.m."

Activity/Workout apps

Some examples of using Siri for fitness-related tasks include:

- "Open the Activity app."
- "Open the Workout app."
- "See Move information in Activity."
- "See Stand information in Activity."
- "See Exercise information in Activity."
- "Open Indoor Walk in Workout app."
- "What's my heart rate?"

Maps app

Some examples of using Siri for looking for directions or for a local business include:

- "Show my location on a map."
- "Where is my closest coffee shop?"
- "Take me home." See Figure 7-5. Siri might ask you where you live the first time you say this (or it pulls the information from your Contacts).
- "Take me to Grand Central Station."
- "What's my next turn?"
- "Give me directions to Mom's office."
- "Find a gas station."
- "Find the best sushi restaurant in Miami."

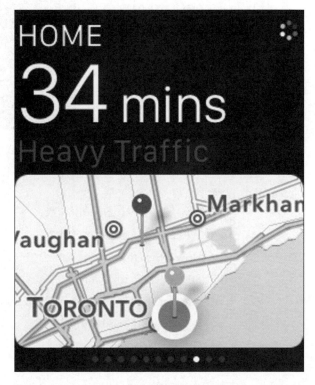

Figure 7-5: Use your voice in the Maps app — perhaps to take you home.

Music app

Some examples of using Siri for playing music include:

- "Play Madonna." (See Figure 7-6.)
- "Play Workout playlist."
- "What song is playing?"
- "Shuffle my music."
- "Play rock music."
- "Play 'Sugar' by Maroon 5."
- "Skip this track."

Miscellaneous

Some other examples of a few other random — but fun — things you can do with Siri on Apple Watch include:

- "What's the weather outside?"
- "What's it going to be like this week?"
- "Do I need a coat?"
- "How are my stocks doing?"
- "What's the Apple stock at?"
- "How's the Dow Jones doing?"
- "Set an alarm for 7 a.m."
- "Set an alarm for one hour from now."
- "Wake me up in 30 minutes."
- "Open Passbook."
- "Open Stopwatch."
- "Open Timer."
- "Open Settings."

Figure 7-6: Ask Siri to play music — whether it's an artist, song, album, genre, playlist, and so on.

Because it takes only a quick Siri request to set up a reminder, you might be tempted to do this while driving. But even a minor distraction could cause an accident, so resist using Apple Watch and Siri until you've parked the car.

Trying Other Tasks With Siri

Siri is one of the fastest, easiest, and most accurate ways to interact with content on your Apple Watch. But Siri can perform lesser-known yet impressive feats too — and the following are some of my favorites.

Setting reminders by location

It's a breeze to ask Siri to remind you of something by time — such as "Tomorrow at 10 a.m., remind me to call the dentist to book an appointment" — but did you know you can set reminders by location too?

For example, raise your wrist and say "Hey, Siri, remind me to call Mom when I leave here." Whenever you leave wherever you are — such as your office, a coffee shop, or a shopping mall — Siri reminds you to call your mom. Your nearby iPhone's integrated GPS means it's location-aware.

Another example: Say "Remind me to take out the trash when I get home." Because Siri knows where your home is because it's in your iPhone's Contacts app — which you can add if you haven't yet done this; see the "Setting Up Siri on Your Apple Watch" section for more — you won't be reminded of the chore until you pull into the driveway.

Reading your texts

Many Siri users are aware you can dictate your text messages; simply say something like "Hey, Siri, text Mary Smith 'Please don't forget to call the florist for tomorrow's event.'"

But did you know you can have your text messages read to you? Raise your wrist or press the Digital Crown button and then say something like "Read my texts." Once Siri reads a message to you, you can say something like "Reply saying 'That's an excellent idea — thanks'" or "Tell her I'll be there in 20 minutes."

You can also ask Siri something like "Do I have any texts from Mary?"

Calculating numbers

Siri includes support from Wolfram Alpha's vast database of facts, definitions, and even pop culture information. (For example, ask Siri who shot J.R. or Mr. Burns!) But you can also ask Siri to perform math problems for you.

If you're adding up checks to deposit at the bank, for example, ask Siri something like "What's $140.40 plus $245.12 plus $742.30 plus $472.90?" and within a moment, you should hear the correct answer (which is $1,600.72).

If you're out with friends at a restaurant and the bill comes to, say, $200, you can also ask Siri something like "What's an 18 percent tip on $200?" and Siri tells you how much that is ($36).

Of course, Siri can also handle multiplication, subtraction, equations, fractions, and more. All you have to do is ask!

Finding your friends

If you're not familiar with the free Find My Friends app on iPhone, it uses GPS to provide your geographical location to people you choose to share this information with, such as a spouse, kids, grandkids, friends, or coworkers. Once you add consensual people to your Friends ring, you can also see their whereabouts on a map — represented by a colored orb — and get the address they're at if desired.

You probably saw this one coming: You can use Siri to get the most from the Find My Friends app. Raise your wrist and say "Hey, Siri, where are my friends?" This opens Find My Friends on your iPhone, and you should see who's around and how far they are from you. Now you can send someone a message, such as "Let's grab a coffee" on your phone. You can also ask Siri something like "Is my husband at home?" or "Where's John Smith?" or "Find my sister." But note that Apple Watch doesn't have a Find My Friends app. You have to pull out your phone for that.

Extending the Fun (and Silly) Ways to Interact With Siri

Siri is also pretty funny — if you haven't yet figured this out from talking to it on your iPhone. In case you haven't, the following are some fun and cheeky things you can ask Siri for on your Apple Watch — and the kinds of responses you can expect.

Spoiler alert: Only read the **bold** questions and not the answers if you want to see what Siri replies with on your own!

Say: "What's the best smartwatch?"

You don't expect Siri to recommend a rival Android-powered watch, do you? Instead, it answers this question with "The Apple Watch will show you a really good time" or "I say Apple Watch — hands down" or another answer.

Say: "I love you, Siri."

Deep down, Siri might be flattered, but it suggests otherwise. Siri might write something like "You hardly know me" or "That's nice — can we get back to work now?" or "Impossible!"

Say: "Siri, I'm bored."

If you find yourself bored while wearing your Apple Watch, you can tell Siri how you're feeling and it replies with something like "Not with me, I hope." Or it'll converse with you — be it offering a story, song lyrics, or a poem or engaging in a "knock, knock" exchange if it's in the mood.

Say: "Who's your daddy?"

This one borders on the naughty. While Siri was a little reluctant at first, it knows which side its bread is buttered. You might hear "You are" or perhaps something like "I know this must mean something — everybody keeps asking me this question."

Say: "What's the meaning of life?"

You can ask Siri a profound question, such as "What's the meaning of life?" and while it might give you a literal translation, you might also see a reply with something cheeky, such as "A movie" or "All evidence to date suggests it's chocolate." Or "I don't know, but I think there's an app for that."

Say: "Will you marry me?"

After professing my affection for Siri (it writes "That's sweet," "I sure have received a lot of marriage proposals lately," or "You are the wind beneath my wings"), I went for it and asked for Siri's, uh, hand in marriage. It's reply: "Let's just be friends, okay?"

8

Fitness Fun: Whipping Yourself Into Shape With Apple Watch

. . . .

In This Chapter

▶ Mastering the Activity app

▶ Navigating the Workout app

▶ Understanding personalized reminders, feedback, and rewards

▶ Reviewing your physical activity and earning rewards

▶ Using Apple Watch's heart rate sensor

. . . .

*F*itness is one of the smartest applications on your smartwatch. Whether you're trying to monitor your regular daily activity, you're determined to lose weight, or you simply want to manage your workout regimes in an easy way, Apple Watch can handle it all. This is also true for athletes looking to maximize their training.

But how does this work, you ask?

Apple Watch and other smartwatches as well as dedicated activity trackers — like the Fitbit, Jawbone's UP family, Nike's FuelBand, Garmin's vivofit, the Microsoft Band, and so on — have a built-in accelerometer to count your number of steps, like an old-fashioned pedometer. (Some activity trackers have a built-in altimeter or barometer sensor to also calculate stairs climbed, but Apple Watch doesn't have this.) While you wear one of these gadgets on your wrist, these high-tech yet water- and sweat-resistant devices can give you real-time information, such as total distance traveled, calories burned, and other details.

But Apple Watch also has an integrated heart rate sensor to track your workout's intensity. It also uses your iPhone's GPS to help track how far you've moved.

Speaking of the iPhone, while Apple Watch shows you activity information on its small screen, you can obtain more details and historical information via apps on your iPhone because it's wirelessly synced with the watch.

This chapter covers how Apple Watch can be used for health and fitness, including a close look at two of its main apps: Activity and Workout. I also discuss the integrated heart rate monitor.

Getting Up and Running With the Activity App

 As Apple explains on its website, fitness isn't "just about running, biking, or hitting the gym. It's also about being active throughout the day."

Thus, one of the two main fitness apps on Apple Watch is devoted to your general activity levels during a regular day. This includes such things as walking the dog, chasing after your kids or grandkids, and taking the stairs instead of an escalator or elevator. The aptly named Activity app, as shown in Figure 8-1, keeps track of everything physical you do — and encourages you to keep moving.

Quite simply, the Activity app gives you a visual snapshot of your daily activity. It's broken down into three colored rings:

Figure 8-1: The Activity app shows you multicolored rings based on your movement, exercise, and more.

- **Move:** The reddish-pink ring shows how many calories you've burned by moving.

- **Exercise:** The lime-green ring is for the minutes of brisk activity you've completed that day.

- **Stand:** The baby-blue ring gives you a visual indication of how often you've stood up after sitting or reclining.

Your goal is to complete each ring each day by reaching the suggested amount of exercise per day, as outlined in this chapter. The more solid each ring is, the better you're doing.

The first (main) screen of the Activity app gives you a summary of Move, Exercise, and Stand, but if you swipe to the left, you can access a dedicated screen for each of the Activity meters.

As shown in Figure 8-2, you should see a summary of each Activity section, which explains what you're seeing in this app.

Before you begin any Activity, however, Apple Watch wants to learn a little about you first — namely, your gender, age, height, and weight. In order for the numbers to be accurate — such as estimating your calories burned — the watch needs to know a few things about you. For example, an 8-year-old female burns calories at a different rate than a 65-year-old male.

You only have to do this once, but as shown in Figure 8-3, you need to answer a few questions first with your fingertip.

If you live in the United States, you should see customary unit measurements, such as pounds, but those who live in Canada or the United Kingdom, for example, have to fill out information using the metric system. (Ditto for setting distance — be it in miles or in kilometers.)

Move

Moving is good — even if it's not that fast. Motion helps you burn calories and gets your heart pumping and your blood flowing. The Activity app's Move ring tells you how well you're doing based on your personal active calorie burn goal for the day, as shown in Figure 8-4. For example, the default goal is 600 calories per day, which is a couple hours of walking around a shopping mall. If that's too easy to reach or, on the flipside, too ambitious, you can easily make necessary adjustments to suit your needs. Just press firmly on the Apple Watch screen (Force Touch) and change the Move goal to something more achievable: Press + or – until you see your desired goal.

Figure 8-2: Apple Watch explains how each of the three Activity tabs — Move, Exercise, and Stand — work.

Figure 8-3: Get started by answering some questions about your gender, age, height, and weight.

To use the Move tab in the Activity app, follow these steps:

1. **Press the Digital Crown button to go to the Home screen.**

2. **Tap the Activity icon.**

    You can also raise your wrist and say "Hey, Siri, Activity." Either action launches the Activity app.

3. **Swipe to the left once on the Activity app's main (summary) screen to land on the Move page. Or whatever you're doing on Apple Watch, tell Siri "Show me Move information" to go right to this screen.**

    Move tells you how much you've moved during the day. The large number in the middle of the watch screen is your current estimated calories burned. The small number underneath is your daily goal, while the reddish-pink ring visually shows how close you are to hitting your daily goal.

    You can change your caloric goal in the Activity app by pressing on the watch screen (Digital Touch) and selecting a new goal. Press + or – to set your desired goal. You can also change your Exercise and Stand goals in the same fashion.

4. **Swipe down on the screen to see a History graph with each hour of the day presented and how well you've done per hour (highlighted by a vertical line).**

   The taller the pink-ish bar, the more you moved that hour, as shown in Figure 8-5.

5. **Twist the Digital Crown button to see even more details about your Move time or press the Digital Crown button to return to the Home screen.**

   You can now go about your business.

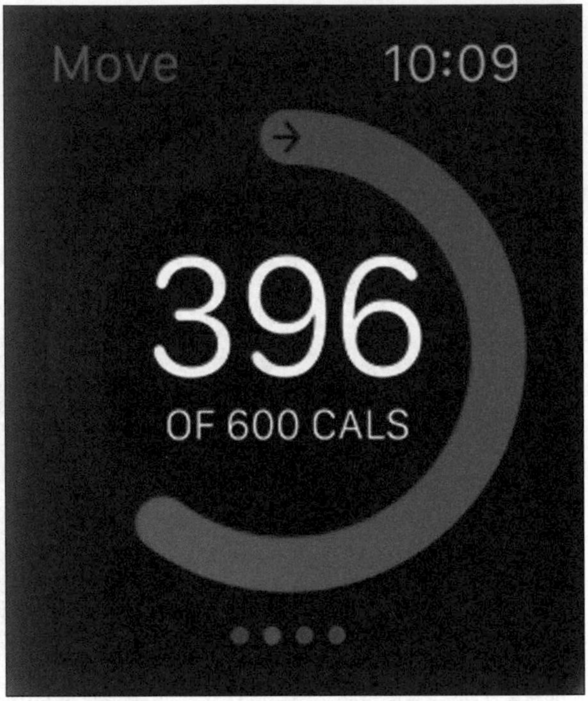

Move   10:09

396
OF 600 CALS

Figure 8-4: Part of the Activity app, Move adds up all the calories you've burned while moving around.

Many different kinds of bands are available for Apple Watch, and active types might prefer the aptly named Sport band made from fluoroelastomer (synthetic rubber), which comes in five different colors. Compared with leather, the link bracelet, and the Milanese loop, the high-performance and smooth Sport band might be most ideal for those who exercise because of its light weight, durability, and resistance to sweat and rain. It also features a pin-and-tuck enclosure for a secure fit. This band is available for all three Apple Watch models. See www.dummies.com/extras/applewatch for more on bands.

Exercise

Whether you want to do something active in one shot — such as jogging on the treadmill after work — or a little bit here and there, it's recommended you do at least 30 minutes of exercise each day. What constitutes "exercise," you ask? How is this different from mere "moving"? Any activity at the level of a brisk walk or above is considered exercise, says Apple. By seeing how much you're exercising — or, rather, not exercising — you might just be motivated to improve your overall health (which has also been proven to be linked to happiness). See Figure 8-6 for a look at the Exercise tab.

To use the Exercise tab in the Activity app, follow these steps:

1. **Press the Digital Crown button to go to the Home screen**

2. **Tap the Activity app.**

   You can also raise your wrist and say "Hey, Siri, Activity." Either action opens the Activity app, taking you to the main Activity screen with a summary of all three rings.

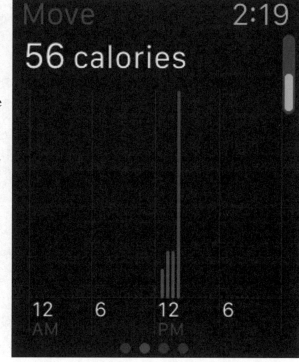

Figure 8-5: Scroll down within the Move tab to see another view of your day's performance — divided by hour.

3. **To go to the Exercise area, swipe twice to the left. Or whatever you're doing on Apple Watch, tell Siri "Show me Exercise information" to go right to this screen.**

   You should see a large number in the middle of the screen. This is the total exercise time calculated for the day so far. Underneath this number is the total goal for the day (such as 30 minutes). The greenish-yellow ring also shows you how close you are to your overall daily goal. To change your goals, press firmly on the screen (Force Touch) and tap + or – to set your desired goal.

4. **Swipe down for your History graph, which shows your hourly activity level — measured in minutes — for when you were most active.**

   As you might expect, the higher the line on the graph, the better. Even if you exercise a little here and a little there, every bit helps and goes toward your daily time goal.

5. **Twist the Digital Crown button for additional exercise information on your Apple Watch, including a numerical summary of your day's achievements. Alternatively, grab your iPhone and open the Activity app.**

6. **Press the Digital Crown button to return to the Home screen.**

Don't be discouraged if you're not reaching your exercise goals. Try again tomorrow or reduce the number of your suggested active minutes — from say 30 minutes to 20 minutes.

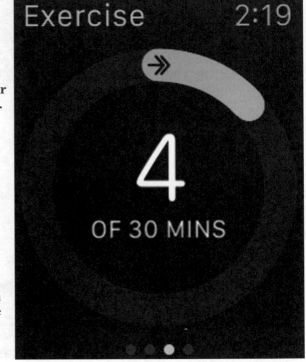

Figure 8-6: The Exercise tab shows you more intense levels of physical activity — such as a brisk walk, jog, or run.

Stand

Many of us — including yours truly — have jobs where we sit for a good chunk of the day. This isn't doing much for those love handles we're trying to get rid of. Apple Watch knows when you stand and move around at least for one minute — and this all goes toward your Stand ring, as shown in Figure 8-7. Even if it's just to get up from your computer and go get a glass of water, a small stretch, or a walk down the hall to say hello to a coworker, all this Stand time adds up. You've completed the default Stand ring requirements if you move at least one minute in 12 different hours during the day. The app also remind you to get up if you've been idle too long (about an hour).

Did you notice the arrows?

You might've missed it, but small arrows inside the rings are associated with each of the three tabs: Move, Exercise, and Stand. The Move app shows an arrow pointing right to imply moving forward; Exercise has a double arrow to suggest more active movement; and Stand has an arrow that points up to confirm it's counting how many times you're rising after sitting.

To use the Stand tab in the Activity app, follow these steps:

1. **Press the Digital Crown button to go to the Home screen.**

2. **Tap the Activity app.**

   You can also raise your wrist and say "Hey, Siri, Activity." Either action opens the Activity app, taking you to the main Activity screen with a summary of all three rings.

3. **Swipe to the left three times to find your Stand information. Or tell Siri "Show me Stand information" to go right to this screen — no matter what you're doing on your watch.**

Figure 8-7: As you can guess by its name, Stand tells you how often you've stood up. You're supposed to do that at least once per hour — 12 times per day.

The first part of the Stand screen shows a large number in the middle of the screen. This shows how many hours you've stood up for (at least one minute per hour). The smaller number underneath the large number is the total goal hours (such as 12). The blue ring visually shows you how you're doing for the day.

Regardless of which Activity screen you're in — the summary page, Move, Exercise, or Stand — you always see a clock in the top-right corner, so you always know the current time without having to leave the Activity app. Smart, no?

4. **Swipe down to open the History graph.**

   You should see the day laid out chronologically and a full vertical bar for any hour you stood (for at least a minute per hour), as shown in Figure 8-8.

   It doesn't matter if it's consecutive hours or spread out throughout the day — the idea is to get up at least once per hour during the day (unless you sleepwalk, which means you won't have to worry about this overnight)!

5. **Twist the Digital Crown button to obtain more information on your activity, such as a numeric summary of your day's progress — including total steps, total distance, and more. (See the "Understanding the Workout App" section for more.)**

Be proud! You're getting your move on.

Understanding the Workout App

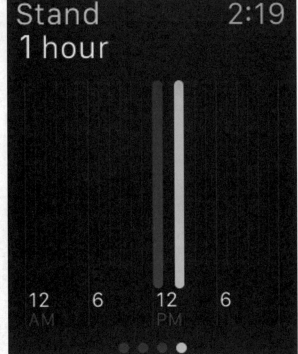

You might be wondering how the Workout app differs from the Activity app. Aren't they the same thing?

Figure 8-8: Apple Watch calculates and displays how often you've stood throughout the day.

Not exactly.

While both are fitness related, the Workout app differs from the Activity app in one respect: Rather than showing your progress over the past day, Workout provides real-time information about calories burned, elapsed time, distance, speed, and pace for your walks, jogs, runs, cycling, and indoor equipment, such as an elliptical, a stair stepper, a rower, a treadmill, and more.

In other words, instead of generic daily stats, the Workout app shows you cardio information based on what you're doing and while you're doing it.

While most activity trackers and smartwatches can spit out generic information on your estimated calories burned — by simply moving — Apple's technology is tailored to specific exercise equipment and/or exercises. All you have to do is choose the type of workout you'd like to tackle — and Apple

Watch turns on the appropriate sensors, such as accelerometer and gyro-scope (for motion), heart rate monitor, and GPS (via your iPhone).

You can then receive a detailed summary of your exercise — and, of course, your workout counts toward your Activity ring measurements for the day.

You can also set goals, chart your progress, and earn awards.

At least not with the first-generation Apple Watch, the Workout app can't be used to track swimming, although the watch is water-resistant (but not water-proof). Why take a chance, no?

To use the Workout app on your Apple Watch, follow these steps:

1. **Press the Digital Crown button to go to the Home screen.**

2. **Tap the Workout app.**

   You can also just raise your wrist and say "Hey, Siri, Workout." Either action launches the Workout app, where you see the main Workout screen. You should see options for many different kinds of indoor and outdoor exercises:

   - Outdoor Walk
   - Outdoor Run
   - Outdoor Cycle
   - Indoor Walk
   - Indoor Run
   - Indoor Cycle
   - Elliptical
   - Rower
   - Stair Stepper
   - Other

3. **Swipe up or down to view a workout or you can cycle through them by twisting the Digital Crown button forward or backward.**

   What are you in the mood for? See Figure 8-9 for some of your options.

Figure 8-9: Choose a workout and tap it to set a goal.

4. **When you see one you like, such as Outdoor Run, tap it to be taken to the goals screen.**

   On this screen, you can select a goal based on:

   - Calories (highlighted in pink)
   - Time (highlighted in yellow)
   - Distance (highlighted in blue)

   See Figure 8-10 for a look at each screen.

5. **Choose one option to set a goal.**

6. **Use your fingertip to press + or – for the numbers to go up or down, respectively.**

   For calories, it might be 300. If you choose a time-based goal, you might select 45 minutes. A distance-based goal might be two miles.

   Remember, you should see different options based on your activity. For example, if you're running indoors, the watch uses the accelerometer, but cycling outdoors uses the GPS on your iPhone to calculate distance. Make sense?

7. **Press Start near the bottom of your screen and then start your workout.**

   Do your thing — and the watch counts your every move. Well, *almost* every move. Remember, Apple Watch might always give you proper credit for things like push-ups, pull-ups, and crunches. Sure, it adds to your Move tab within the Activity app, but it might not help properly calculate your calories burned in the Workout app. But still do them because you know it helps your health — even if your watch doesn't!

   During your workout, you should see progress updates to help motivate you. You should also receive timely encouragement when you've hit halfway toward the end of your workout, for example, or perhaps based on a milestone, such as reaching one mile during a three-mile jog. See Figure 8-11 for an example.

8. **If you need to pause or end your workout, press firmly on the watch screen (Force Touch) to open the screen shown in Figure 8-11 or press the Digital Crown button to return to the Home screen.**

   When you open the Workout app again, you can see the date and time of your best and last workouts — divided by activity (such as Outdoor Walk). You can even see what the weather was like at the time.

Figure 8-10: These numbers are all at zero to start, and you get to select which one(s) you'd like to achieve. Or don't set a goal at all and go for a run; Apple Watch will still calculate your steps, time, distance, and calories burned.

Figure 8-11: An alert about how well you're achieving a goal, such as the one on the left, can help give you incentive to keep going. You can always press the screen to pause or cancel a workout, as shown on the right.

9. **Swipe through the Workout screens to see a summary of your workout, including total calories burned, active calories burned (when you were physically exerting yourself), resting calories burned, average pace per mile, average heart rate, total distance, and total time of workout. Figure 8-12 shows a few of these summary screens after a short walk.**

   To remind you, all the numbers are color coded too, such as your total distance in blue, total time in yellow, and active calories burned in pink. At the bottom of the summary screen, you can choose to Save or Discard this information. Tap which option you prefer.

Now you know how to select, start, and stop a Workout as well as read your summary information. And don't forget: After you review your accomplishments, you can repeat the exercise (with the same goals) to see how you fare or you might decide to increase or decrease the goal. Or choose a different goal altogether. If you started with time or distance, you might change it up to set a goal based on caloric burn.

Figure 8-12: Swipe your fingertip to see a report on your workout session, including distance, calories burned, and heart rate.

Personalizing Reminders, Feedback, and Achievements

Despite what you've heard, information is bliss — not ignorance.

Apple Watch can not only calculate your workouts for you, but it can also present the data in an accessible way so you can see how well (or poorly) you're doing toward reaching your fitness goals. Actually, the watch goes one step further: It can nudge you to be more active, provide weekly goal summaries, and reward you for a job well done.

Reminders

Apple Watch delivers customizable coaching reminders that can help you reach your Activity goals: Move, Exercise, and Stand. You can disable these in the Apple Watch app on the iPhone. Go to Settings⇨Activity.

Along with notifying you to get up when you've been idle for too long, over time, Apple Watch learns your goals and accomplishments and suggests a daily Move goal for the week that's achievable. You can adjust your fitness goals — whether it's bumping them up or trimming them down — to something more reasonable based on your capabilities or time.

Summary

Every Monday, you should receive a weekly check-in, which serves as a summary of your Activity progress. It might say something like this: "Last week's Active Calorie burn goal was 300. You hit it 4 out of 7 days." On the graph that accompanies the text, you can see which days you reached your goal and by how much; the higher the vertical column, the better you did. You should see all seven days of the week presented.

You can also open the Activity app to glimpse how you're doing per day, and you can always swipe down from within the Activity app to see an hour-by-hour account of your daily Move, Exercise, and Stand goals. See the "Getting Up and Running With the Activity App" section as well as the "Using the Activity App on Your iPhone" section for more on the Activity app.

Achievements

Isn't it enough incentive to know you're doing well? Well, not always. Let's face it: It's nice to be acknowledged for your efforts — and even rewarded.

"Get a pat on the back, right on the wrist," says Apple on its website.

I like that.

Earn special badges, such as the ones seen in Figure 8-13 — although they're a little hard to see because I haven't completed them yet and thus they're not colored in. These badges are stored in the Activity app on your iPhone, which you can look at with pride.

Some examples of Move badges include:

- **Perfect Month:** Earn this award when you reach your Move goal every day of a single month — from the month's first day to the last.

- **Move Goal 200%:** Earn this award every time you double your daily Move goal.

- **100 Move Goals:** Earn this award when you reach your daily Move goal 100 times.

More importantly, perhaps it'll encourage you to keep going.

Using the Activity App on Your iPhone

You can only fit so much information on the small Apple Watch. Thus, the Activity app on your iPhone takes it a step further by providing you with a ton of data based on your Move, Exercise, and Stand achievements as well as Workout information.

Specifically, the iPhone app's History tab maps out your progress over long periods of time; you can look at how well you did by day, week, month, or year. See Figure 8-14 for a look at the Activity app on iPhone.

The Activity app also displays your badges (of honor!) as well as an Achievements tab that shows you various objectives to unlock as added incentives. Like many video games that reward you for achieving goals — such as "Complete an end-level boss fight in under five minutes" or "Capture a town without losing a life" — your Activity app can also give you fitness-related challenges to take on. By default, the app has a dozen challenges — each represented by a badge-like icon, which could be "Reach your Move, Exercise, and Stand goals in one day" or "Exercise a total of 20 miles."

What's more, the Activity app syncs its data with your iPhone's Health app, where it can be accessed by third-party health and fitness apps — with your permission of course.

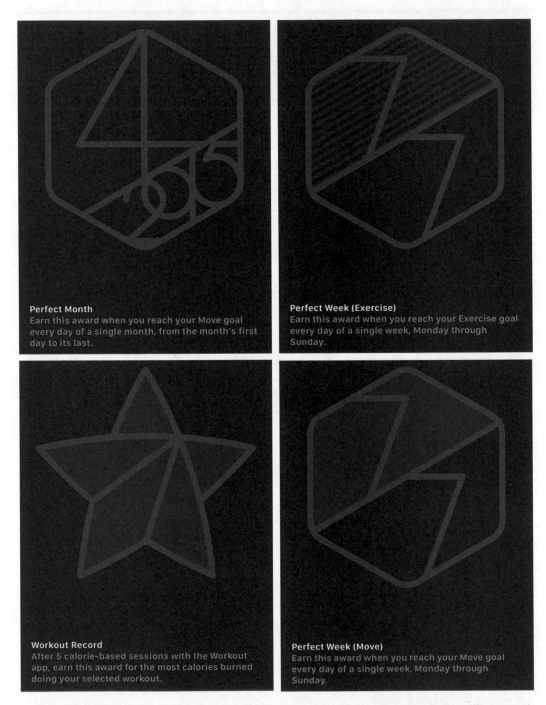

Perfect Month
Earn this award when you reach your Move goal every day of a single month, from the month's first day to its last.

Perfect Week (Exercise)
Earn this award when you reach your Exercise goal every day of a single week, Monday through Sunday.

Workout Record
After 5 calorie-based sessions with the Workout app, earn this award for the most calories burned doing your selected workout.

Perfect Week (Move)
Earn this award when you reach your Move goal every day of a single week, Monday through Sunday.

Figure 8-13: A look at some of the Apple Watch badges you can earn for reaching a milestone. These aren't filled out yet (author hangs his head in shame) or else the award emblems would be colored in.

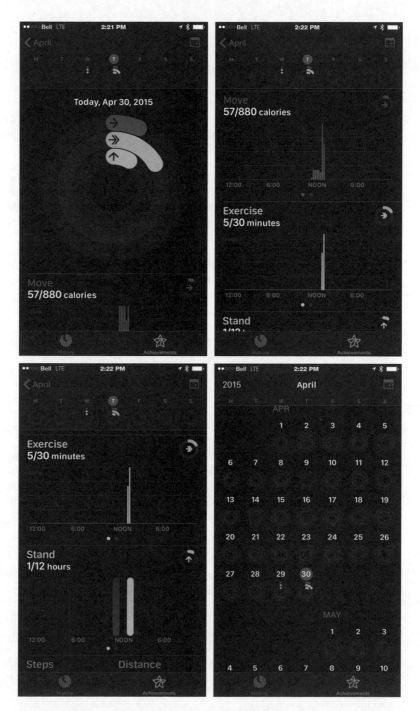

Figure 8-14: A look at the Activity app — on your iPhone — with this weekly summary of your Activity levels.

Understanding Apple Watch's Heart Rate Monitor

Underneath the Apple Watch case — the part that touches your skin — is a ceramic cover with sapphire lenses. Beneath that is a series of small sensors, which can give you a slight vibration to tell you something (Apple's Taptic Engine), but also a heart rate monitor to give you an idea about the intensity of your workout — or simply your resting heart rate.

The heart rate sensor uses infrared (IR) and visible-light LEDs (light-emitting diodes) and photodiodes to detect your heart rate — measured in beats per minute (BPM). The average heart rate is 72 BPM, but when you start your workout and your muscles need more oxygen, your heart beats faster to pump oxygen-filled blood throughout your body.

Every ten minutes, Apple Watch measures your heart rate and stores that information in the iPhone's Health app. This data, along with other information it collects about your movement, goes toward estimating the number of calories you're burning.

On how the heart rate sensor works, Apple explains on its website that it uses what is known as "photoplethysmography." "This technology, while difficult to pronounce, is based on a very simple fact: Blood is red because it reflects red light and absorbs green light." Apple Watch uses green LED lights, paired with light-sensitive photodiodes, to detect the amount of blood flowing through your wrist. "When your heart beats, the blood flow in your wrist — and the green light absorption — is greater," says Apple.

By flashing its LED lights — in an alternating fashion and hundreds of times per second — Apple Watch calculates the number of times the heart beats per minute. Apple says its heart rate sensor can also use infrared light, which is what it uses when it measures your heart rate every ten minutes. But if this infrared system isn't giving a reliable reading, your smartwatch switches to the green LEDs.

If someone you know also has an Apple Watch, you can send him or her your heartbeat. See Chapter 5 for more about how to do this — as well as send taps and sketches to other Apple Watch owners.

For the heart rate monitor to work effectively, Apple Watch must be worn with a snug fit. For example, if your watch band is too loose, the back of the watch case might not touch your skin enough or might move around during a reading. For all the bands available with Apple Watch, you can tighten it a bit if need be. See www.dummies.com/extras/applewatch for more on Apple Watch bands.

Other factors can also affect a reading, such as weather — readings might be off if it's too cold out — as well as fast or constant movement that can jostle the watch around too much for an accurate heart rate measurement, such as an intense game of squash. And some people just don't give a good reading at all. It happens.

If you're not getting a good reading — some Apple Watch owners with major tattoos say the heart rate monitor won't work, for example — don't forget that Apple Watch and iPhone can work with external heart rate monitors, such as a chest strap, using wireless Bluetooth technology.

9

Mucho Media: Managing Your Music, Movies, and More

In This Chapter
▶ Managing music from your wrist
▶ Using Siri to play your music
▶ Pairing Bluetooth headphones with Apple Watch
▶ Listening to music on your Apple Watch
▶ Playing podcasts, audiobooks, and radio plays
▶ Using Apple Watch to control Apple TV
▶ Accessing your iTunes library with your watch

Music lovers, listen up. Your Apple Watch can help you get more from your favorite tunes.

In this chapter, I cover how to use Apple Watch to control music on your iPhone, allowing you to keep your phone tucked away but to be able to navigate through all the tracks on your wrist while you're on the go.

But you don't even need your iPhone to listen to music. Your Apple Watch can also store and play music for those times you don't want to bring your iPhone with you — as long as you have Bluetooth headphones with which to listen. I show you how to do that too.

I also discuss how to control your music hands-free — as well as audiobooks, podcasts, and radio plays — by using Siri.

While not widely publicized, Apple Watch can also be used to control your Apple TV connected to your TV or your iTunes library on your PC or Mac.

Accessing — and Mastering — the Music App

Similar to the iPhone app, Apple Watch has a Music app that lets you find and play music stored on your iPhone.

Sure, you can also install music on the Apple Watch itself — something I cover later in this chapter in the "Playing Music From Your Apple Watch" section — but most wearers will likely use their watch as a kind of wireless remote control.

Sample scenario: You're walking down the street with your swank Beats by Dr. Dre headphones plugged into your iPhone. Rather than taking the phone out of your jeans every time you want to switch tracks or choose a playlist, lift your arm and perform those functions from the comfort of your wrist. Apple Watch is all about convenience — glanceable information when and where you need it — and controlling music is no different.

To manage your iPhone music from your Apple Watch, follow these steps:

1. **Press the Digital Crown button to go to the Home screen.**

2. **Tap the Music app.**

   Alternatively, swipe up to open your Glances while in the Clock app. The Music Glance should be the first one you see (before swiping to the left to see other apps). This Music Glance screen shows you the current track playing on your iPhone, as shown in Figure 9-1.

   You can also raise your wrist and say "Hey, Siri, play Music" or something else specific.

   On this Music screen, you should see the name of the song, the artist, and the album artwork (if available). If a song is already playing

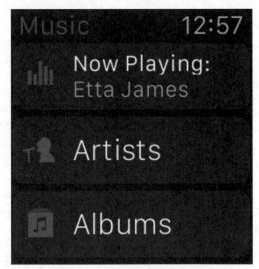

Figure 9-1: Swipe left inside the Music app and select how you'd like to find and play your music.

on your iPhone, you should see small equalizer bars dance at the top of the screen and some scrolling information, such as the complete name of the track, the album name, and more.

3. **Tap the triangular Play button to play the song — if it isn't already playing — which you should hear through your iPhone, wired earbuds/headphones, or Bluetooth headset.**

   Remember, you can't hear music through Apple Watch — nor would you want to — unless you have a Bluetooth headset or headphones. By default, music plays on your iPhone, but if you have a Bluetooth device, see the "Pairing a Bluetooth Device With Apple Watch" for how to add one to your Apple Watch.

4. **Tap + or – to increase or decrease the volume, respectively.**

   A red horizontal bar visually shows you how loud the volume is getting. You can also skip forward or backward between tracks by using the double arrows on each side of the Play button. The elapsed time of the track is in the top-left corner and a digital clock is in the top-right corner.

But what do you do if you want to hear a new song? You've got many options on how to handle that. If you swipe to the left inside the Music app, you can bring up a menu that segregates your music collection into various categories. Keep in mind that not all the categories can be seen on the screen at the same time, so you need to scroll up and down

When you swipe through the Music app, you can see five basic pieces of information about your music — discussed in the following sections.

Now Playing

This shows you the artist that's currently playing. You can tap this to bring the track up full screen, to pause the song, or to perhaps skip back to play the song again from the beginning. If no album art has been imported for this track, as recognized by iTunes, this area will just have text and the virtual control buttons, as shown in Figure 9-2.

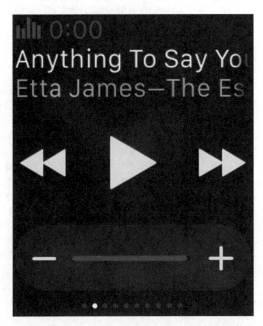

Figure 9-2: No album art? No worries. You should still see pertinent information about a song.

Artists

You can see your music collection listed alphabetically by artist/band. Swipe up or down with your fingertip or twist the Digital Crown button at the speed of your choosing to review the list. As shown in Figure 9-3, under each artist, you should see how many songs you have from that person or band.

Albums

As you might expect, this is where you can see all your music listed alphabetically by album name. This is ideal for when you want to hear an entire album from the same artist or one or more tracks from an album or perhaps a compilation or movie soundtrack with multiple artists.

Songs

As shown in Figure 9-4, this is where you can find all your songs listed alphabetically — regardless of artist. Swipe up or down using your fingertip or twist the Digital Crown button to find something to listen to. Be aware, choosing to see your music collection by song yields the longest list, as you should see by the small bar on the top-right side of the screen when you start to use the Digital Crown button to scroll up or down.

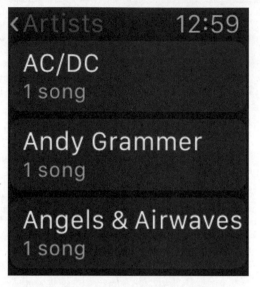

Figure 9-3: The Artists view inside the Music app on Apple Watch.

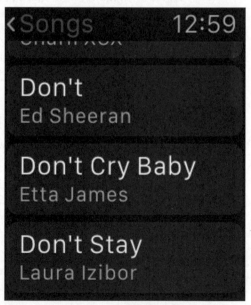

Figure 9-4: Swipe or twist the Digital Crown button to scroll up and down your list of tracks.

Playlists

This shows all your music grouped in some fashion — whether by theme, event, or genre, as shown in Figure 9-5. You can do this in iTunes (on your PC or Mac) or on your iPhone or iPad. You might call a playlist something like "Driving Tunes," "Workout Mix," "Relaxing Music," or whatever suits your fancy. If you have a playlist on your iOS device, then you should see it on your synced Apple Watch.

You can also sync a playlist to the watch to listen to media when no iPhone is around. See the "Playing Music From Your Apple Watch" section for more on syncing playlists.

Keep in mind that while you can access a playlist on Apple Watch, you can't create a playlist on it. For that, you have to sync via iTunes or your iPhone.

You can also use Force Touch to bring up additional options. To use Force Touch on your Apple Watch, follow these steps:

1. **While listening to a track, press firmly on the screen (Force Touch) to open a submenu.**

   You should now see four options presented to you on the Apple Watch screen: Shuffle, Repeat, Source, and AirPlay, as shown in Figure 9-6.

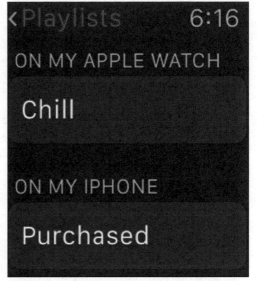

Figure 9-5: You can't create a new playlist like you can on your iPhone or in iTunes, but you can play it on your Apple Watch. Or you can even store the playlist on the watch if an iPhone isn't nearby.

Figure 9-6: These song options should be familiar to iPhone and iPad users.

2. **Tap Shuffle to shuffle all the music on your iPhone.**

   In case you're not familiar with the term, this popular option plays your music in a random order (and different each time), which is akin to shuffling cards in a deck. Those two intertwined arrows on the icon is the international symbol for *Shuffle*. Seriously. Google it.

3. **Tap Repeat to play the same song, album, or playlist again.**

   This icon plays selected track(s) over again.

4. **Tap Source when you want to switch between music playing on your iPhone (default setting) and what might be stored on your Apple Watch's internal memory.**

   You can't tap this icon if you don't have any music stored on your Apple Watch.

5. **Tap AirPlay to wirelessly play music through an AirPlay-enabled speaker or Apple TV device.**

   Unlike Bluetooth, which might be more universal, AirPlay is Apple's proprietary wireless streaming technology, and it offers better sound — as long as you're on a Wi-Fi network.

Having Siri Play Your Music

Do you know what's even faster than tapping and scrolling to find music? Asking Siri to play it for you.

Say you're itching to hear a song in your collection that's been stuck in your head all day. Or maybe you want to give your favorite band's new greatest hits album a spin from beginning to end? All you need to do is ask Siri (politely) to play an individual song or album.

As long as you're in a place you can talk freely, Siri can launch a song, album, artist, playlist, or genre — just by your asking for it.

To have Siri help you play your music via Apple Watch, raise your wrist and say "Hey, Siri, play _____ (name of song, artist, playlist, and so on)." Or press and hold the Digital Crown button to activate Siri. Ask away!

After Siri processes your request — and don't forget, you need cellular or Wi-Fi access for this to work — you should see and hear the music you asked for via your iPhone (or, if only stored on Apple Watch, through Bluetooth headphones).

Some examples of what you can ask Siri to play:

- ✐ "Play 'Take Me to Church.'" (individual song)
- ✐ "Play Katy Perry." (artist)
- ✐ "Play 'Road Trip' playlist." (specific playlist)
- ✐ "Play some hip-hop." (genre)
- ✐ "Shuffle my music." (shuffling all tracks)
- ✐ "Shuffle James Brown." (shuffling tracks by a certain artist)
- ✐ "What song is this?" or "Who is this?" (Siri shows and/or tells you.)
- ✐ "Play similar music." (to play similar music to what you're listening to)

You can also control your music with your voice. The following are some commands you can give to take control over your tunes via your voice. Press and hold the Digital Crown button (or raise your arm and say "Hey, Siri"), followed by:

- ✐ **"Play"** to play the song shown on your watch screen.
- ✐ **"Pause"** to pause the track you're listening to.
- ✐ **"Skip"** to go to the next track.
- ✐ **"Next"** to (also) go to the next track.
- ✐ **"Previous song"** or **"Play previous song"** to have Siri play the previously played song.

Pairing a Bluetooth Device With Apple Watch

You can load up your watch with music (see the "Playing Music From Your Apple Watch" section) and take it to go — but there's one catch. You can't listen to music through the Apple Watch's tiny speaker (nor would you want to), and there's no headphone jack to plug in headphones.

Instead, you need to pair Bluetooth headphones (or a speaker) to Apple Watch in order to hear music.

To clarify, this isn't necessary if your iPhone is nearby because you should hear music coming from the iPhone's speakers or from headphones connected to the iPhone. Pairing a Bluetooth device with Apple Watch directly is only required if your iPhone isn't around.

To connect a Bluetooth device to your Apple Watch, follow these steps:

1. **Put your Bluetooth headphones or speaker in pairing mode.**

   You might see a flashing light on the device to confirm it's awaiting a connection. It's different for all products, but pairing usually involves pressing and holding the Home button until you see a flashing light.

2. **On Apple Watch, locate the Settings app — which looks like a gray gear — and tap it.**

   Alternatively, you can lift your wrist and say "Hey, Siri, Settings."

3. **Inside Settings, twist the Digital Crown button until you locate Bluetooth and then tap this option.**

   Wait a moment and your Bluetooth headphones or speakers should appear in this list.

4. **Select the Bluetooth device you want to pair it with by tapping its name with your fingertip. Figure 9-7 shows Apple Watch searching for a device, but after a device appears, you can tap it.**

   You've successfully paired the device, but you still need to change the music source from iPhone to Apple Watch to hear music come from your Bluetooth-enabled headphones, which you can learn about in the "Playing Music From Your Apple Watch" section.

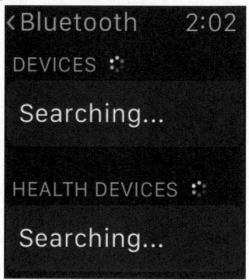

Figure 9-7: Pair a Bluetooth device to hear synced music on your Apple Watch — if no iPhone is nearby.

Playing Music From Your Apple Watch

Not all smartwatches let you store music on your wrist, so you don't need a nearby smartphone, but Apple Watch does indeed offer this feature.

After all, sometimes, you might not have your phone with you, such as when you go out for a jog for a few minutes, so why shouldn't you be able to listen to your favorite high-energy music to keep you pumped up?

But this convenience comes with two limitations:

- ✔ **Sound:** For one, Apple Watch has no headphone jack; therefore, you need a pair of Bluetooth headphones wirelessly paired with your smart-watch — as discussed in the "Pairing a Bluetooth Device With Apple Watch" section — in order to hear anything stored on it.

- ✔ **Space:** You have some storage allocated for music and probably enough for many songs, but that space is considerably smaller than what your iPhone, iPad, and computer have. Specifically, you've got up to 2 giga-bytes of internal storage on Apple Watch, which is the equivalent of about 500 songs (at roughly 4 megabytes each).

After you accept these caveats, follow these steps to transfer music to your Apple Watch from an iPhone:

1. **Connect your Apple Watch to your PC or Mac via its USB charger.**

   Use the special magnetic charger that shipped with your Apple Watch.

2. **On your iPhone, open the Apple Watch app.**

3. **Under My Watch, scroll down and tap Music.**

   Music is the red icon with a white music note on it. You have to scroll down a bit once the Music screen opens because of many settings here, as shown in Figure 9-8, along with apps installed on your Apple Watch.

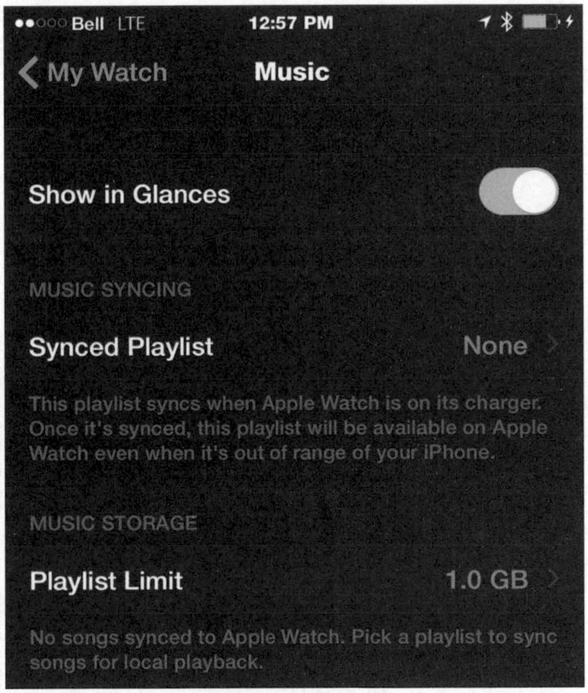

Figure 9-8: You need your iPhone to sync music to Apple Watch. This image shows how to select a playlist on the iPhone app.

4. **Under Synced Playlist, tap the word None to change it and then choose the one you'd like from the list of options.**

Those options include:

* My Top Rated

* Recently Added

* Recently Played

* Top 25 Most Played

* Purchased

You should also see custom-made playlists you've already created on your iPhone or iTunes (such as "Awesome Driving Tunes," "90s Grunge," or "Reggae Mix"). Based on which selection you make, the relevant songs are transferred to your Apple Watch. You should see the words Sync Pending and then Synced. Keep in mind that the more songs you synchronize, the longer it takes to copy them to Apple Watch.

Don't worry about transferring too many tunes over to Apple Watch because Apple won't let you go over your allotted storage of 2 gigabytes.

Have songs stored on your Apple Watch? To listen to music on your Apple Watch rather than your iPhone, follow these steps:

1. **Press and hold the Apple Watch screen (Force Touch) while in the Music app to launch a couple options.**

You should see options for Shuffle, Repeat, AirPlay, and Device.

2. **Tap Device and you should see you're able to toggle between your devices.**

It says: "Choose a music source to play from: iPhone and Apple Watch."

3. **Select Apple Watch, as shown in Figure 9-9.**

After you tap Apple Watch, the screen should say "Pair a Bluetooth headset to listen to music on your Apple Watch."

Figure 9-9: You need to select Apple Watch as your music source to hear music when your iPhone isn't around.

4. **Tap Settings and then choose a paired device from the list. Pick the one you've got with you.**

Now you're ready to rock, roll, dance, swing, or relax.

Playing Podcasts, Audiobooks, and Radio Plays

Apple Watch doesn't have an app to allow you to play podcasts, audiobooks, or radio plays — at least not at the time of my writing *Apple Watch For Dummies* — but that doesn't mean you can't control and listen to them on your watch.

Simply treat these other forms of audio entertainment as songs, such as making a playlist in iTunes (on a computer) or on your iPhone, and then choose to sync it to your Apple Watch to listen to it when you don't have your iPhone around.

Podcasts

Podcasts (a word that fuses iPod with broadcasting) are free downloadable programs from the Internet — be it a comedy routine, a news report, a political rant, cooking instructions, tech advice, gardening tips, a religious sermon, or the latest music remix from a popular DJ.

Many podcasts have video, but here, I'm only referring to the audio-based ones.

In iTunes, click the Podcasts tab and then take a look at the Top Episodes, Top Podcasts, Editor's Choice, and New & Noteworthy or click Categories to choose a specific theme. Click to play a podcast right in iTunes.

If you hear a podcast you like, you can subscribe with the simple click of the mouse; every time a new show is available, you can have it automatically download to your computer's hard drive (or phone's internal memory).

Unlike your favorite local radio station, podcasts let you to choose when the program starts (called *time shifting*) and where you want to listen to it — even in another country (called *place shifting*).

Anyone can publish a podcast — be it a 16-year-old video game fan or huge media corporations, such as ABC/Disney, CNN, or HBO. Thousands of radio stations have podcasts of their popular programs.

Best of all, they're free.

After podcasts are downloaded to your computer, you can use the Apple Watch handoff feature to play them from Apple Watch. See Chapter 5 for more on the handoff feature.

Or you can sync them to your Apple Watch if desired. You do need to be a little tech-savvy to pull it off though.

To sync podcasts to your Apple Watch, follow these steps:

1. **On your computer, open up the iTunes directory in Windows Explorer (for PCs) or Finder (in Macs). On Windows PCs, for example, the directory will be under Music ⇨ iTunes ⇨ iTunes Media ⇨ Podcasts.**

   Inside this directory, you should see all your podcasts as folders, and inside each folder, you should find the individual podcast episodes as .MP3 audio tracks.

2. **Launch iTunes and click the Music tab.**

   In the top-left corner, you should see a little icon with an arrow.

3. **Click this icon to bring up some options, including New.**

4. **Click New with your mouse, followed by New Playlist.**

   Give a name to your Podcasts Playlist, such as "Podcasts" or perhaps the name of the podcast, such as "Star Talk" (one of my faves!).

5. **Drag and drop the podcasts (MP3s) from Windows Explorer or Finder into this newly created playlist.**

   Now you're ready to sync your new playlist over to Apple Watch so you can hear your podcasts without a nearby iPhone.

Learn more about podcasts here: www.apple.com/ca/itunes/podcasts.

Audiobooks

Call audiobooks today's answer to books on tape — if you're old enough to remember those.

As you might expect, audiobooks are usually spoken versions of books — by a narrator — as if you were being read a bedtime story. This differs from a radio play, which I discuss in the "Radio Plays" section, which is acted out by a cast and often with sound effects and music.

You can download millions of audiobooks from the Internet, including from within iTunes, but unlike podcasts and radio plays, they're usually not free. Still, they're a great way to have a book read to you — if you're visually impaired, if you want to make a long commute in the car (or on the bus or train) a more enjoyable one, or if you have trouble reading and would simply rather hear someone read to you.

Audiobooks are available for new books (including *New York Times* bestsellers) as well as slightly older and even classic titles. It doesn't matter if it's fiction or nonfiction; chances are, you can find an audiobook version of a paperback or hardcover book and many electronic books (ebooks) too.

Be aware, however, that copying a downloaded audiobook to a music folder in iTunes — to make it easier to control and play on an Apple Watch — might be a bit more difficult if the audiobook has digital rights management (DRM) encryption on the file, which might limit or prevent it from being copied to another device. DRM protects the copyright owner to help reduce piracy, which is the unauthorized distribution and/or duplication of copyrighted material.

Many thousands of human-read or computer-generated audiobooks based on classic works are freely available in the public domain, and you can copy them over to Apple Watch. You won't find many of these kinds of audiobooks in iTunes, so if you want to copy these freely (and legitimately) available audiobooks to Apple Watch, find them from such websites as Loyal Books, LibriVox, Project Gutenberg, and AudioBooksForFree.com.

After you've downloaded the audio files — usually MP3s — to your hard drive, follow these steps to sync them to your Apple Watch:

1. **Launch iTunes and click the Music tab.**

   In the top-left corner, you should see a little icon with an arrow.

2. **Click this icon to bring up some options, including New.**

3. **Click New with your mouse, followed by New Playlist.**

   Give a name to your audiobooks playlist, such as "Audiobooks."

4. **Wherever you downloaded the DRM-free audiobooks to your computer — maybe your desktop or a Downloads directory — drag and drop them into this newly created playlist.**

   Now you're ready to sync your new playlist over to Apple Watch so you can hear your audiobook(s) without a nearby iPhone.

Learn more about audiobooks here: itunes.apple.com/us/genre/audiobooks.

Radio plays

If you're listening to only music on your iPhone, iPad, or Apple Watch, you're missing out on many thousands of downloadable and free dramas and comedies to help keep you entertained while on the go.

Popularized in the 1940s before TV took off, radio plays — or old-time radio (OTR) shows, as they're often referred to today — are enjoying a 21st-century rebirth thanks to the Internet and MP3s. A whole new generation of listeners can now experience these wonderfully written and performed "theater of the mind" episodes.

Recommended shows include the creepy *Inner Sanctum* and *The Price of Fear* (with Vincent Price) mysteries; nail-biting adventures from *Suspense* and *Escape*; the hilarious antics of Jack Benny as well as Abbott and Costello; and such sci-fi classics as *Journey Into Space* and *X Minus One* (featuring many Ray Bradbury yarns).

Filling up your digital devices with these timeless tales is as easy as subscribing to one of the many dozen OTR podcasts (some with daily updates) or by bookmarking such websites as `Archive.org` and `OTRCat.com` — each with thousands of free downloadable episodes.

Because most of these older shows have copyrights that have long since expired (or didn't have any to begin with), they're now available for free through the public domain. Some are newer, such as many BBC radio plays and recently published radio dramas based on *The Twilight Zone*, and are still protected by copyrights that prohibit you from copying and distributing them. When in doubt, contact the website that houses these audio plays.

To sync radio plays to your Apple Watch, follow these steps:

1. **Launch iTunes and click the Music tab.**

   In the top-left corner, you should see a little icon with an arrow.

2. **Click this icon to bring up some options, including New.**

3. **Click New with your mouse, followed by New Playlist.**

   Give a name to your Radio Shows Playlist, such as "Radio Shows" or "OTR," or by name, such as "Inner Sanctum" or "Suspense."

4. **Wherever you downloaded the radio shows on your computer — maybe your desktop or a Downloads directory — drag and drop them into this newly created playlist.**

   Now you're ready to sync your new playlist over to Apple Watch so you can hear your radio plays without a nearby iPhone.

Now you can look forward to — rather than dread — your daily commute.

Controlling Apple TV and iTunes With Your Apple Watch

Your fancy schmancy new Apple Watch can control your iPhone wirelessly, such as playing music or snapping the shutter on your iPhone's camera (see Chapter 12), but it can also let you manage your Apple TV box connected to your TV and your iTunes software installed on a Windows PC or Mac.

With the latter, the Remote app lets you play back content on your computer as if it were a TV — as long as the media is in your iTunes library. Put that mouse away and start controlling iTunes from your wrist. Or maybe you're cooking in the other room and you want to change music pumping from the speaker? No need to physically go to your laptop or desktop.

Before you can control iTunes or Apple TV, though, you first need to set up Home Sharing in iTunes and sign in with your Apple ID.

To set up Home Sharing in iTunes, follow these steps:

1. **Download the free Remote app from the App Store.**

2. **On your computer, open up iTunes and click the little rectangular icon in the very top-left corner of the screen.**

3. **Click Preferences.**

   A number of tabs appear across the top of this Preferences window.

4. **Click the blue Sharing tab and select what media you'd like to share via Home Sharing.**

   Options include Music, Movies, Home Videos, TV Shows, Podcasts, iTunes U, Books, Purchased, and others.

5. **Now connect your devices, such as iPad and iPhone, to your home Wi-Fi network and then sign in to Home Sharing via the Remote app.**

   Home Sharing is now enabled on iTunes.

Apple TV

To control Apple TV from your Apple Watch, follow these steps:

1. **Press the Digital Crown button to go to the Home screen.**

2. **Tap the Remote app.**

   You can also raise your wrist and say "Hey, Siri, Remote." Either action launches the Remote app. You're presented with two options: Apple TV and iTunes.

3. **Select Apple TV if you own one of these media boxes and it's attached to your TV.**

   As long as your iPhone and Apple TV box are joined to the same wireless (Wi-Fi) network at home or work, you can access your Apple TV as if your Apple Watch were that small remote control that comes with it. (You can also control Apple TV with the Remote app for iOS — for the iPhone, iPod touch, and iPad — if you'd like to.)

4. **Tap one of the four arrows on the watch — Up, Down, Right, or Left — to navigate Apple TV's menus.**

No more reaching for the hardware remote or phone or tablet; controlling your media can now be done with a tap on your wrist.

5. **Tap the center Play/Pause button to stop and start your media at your convenience.**

You're at home, with your feet up on the coffee table, and you're enjoying a bit of Netflix on your big screen — until your dog brings you a leash in its mouth (and with those sad eyes). Tap the center of your Apple Watch to pause playback and then take your pup for a walk.

6. **Press the Digital Crown button to return to the Home screen.**

And don't forget to turn off your TV and Apple TV box if you're done. Don't waste power and money.

iTunes

To control iTunes from your Apple Watch, follow these steps:

1. **Tap the Digital Crown button to go to the Home screen.**

2. **Tap the Remote app.**

You can also raise your wrist and say "Hey, Siri, Remote." Either action launches the Remote app.

3. **Inside the app, tap iTunes.**

You're prompted to type in a four-digit code to access your iTunes library. And remember, you need to be connected to the same Wi-Fi network as your Mac or Windows PC and be signed into Home Sharing in iTunes (as covered earlier in this section).

4. **Swipe around the Apple Watch screen to access the library of content on iTunes and then select something to play.**

The Remote app lets you control your iTunes library from anywhere in your home. Fast-forward, pause, or skip back a track or two. Choose a song, shuffle an album, or select a custom playlist. And if your Mac or PC is sleeping, opening the Remote app wakes it up.

10

Pay for Play: Making Mobile Payments With Apple Watch

· ·

In This Chapter

▶ Understanding Apple Pay

▶ Using Apple Pay on Apple Watch

▶ Setting up Apple Watch for Apple Pay

▶ Paying with Apple Watch without a nearby iPhone

▶ Accessing Passbook on Apple Watch

▶ Using Apple Watch for deals and rewards

· ·

This chapter looks at how to use Apple Pay on Apple Watch. First, though, a brief primer on what Apple Pay is.

If you own an iPhone 6 or newer, then perhaps you've had a chance to try out Apple Pay (www.apple.com/apple-pay) — Apple's proprietary mobile payment solution that lets you buy goods and services without needing your wallet.

Simply wave your compatible phone over a contactless terminal at a participating retailer — with your finger or thumb on the Touch ID sensor (built into the Home button) — and the transaction is completed. This saves time at retail because you don't have to dig for the exact change or deal with finding the right credit or debit card in your wallet.

Because of the integrated near field communication (NFC) antenna in the latest iPhones, you don't need to open an app or even wake up your phone to use it. You don't even need to look at your phone. As long as your one-of-a-kind fingerprint (or thumbprint) is detected on the Home button — an example of biometrics technology that proves it's you and only you — you should feel a subtle vibration and hear a small beep to confirm the *digital handshake* has been made.

If you're worried about security, Apple Pay doesn't disclose your financial information to the retailer; a unique numerical *token* is used instead of actual credit or debit card numbers exchanged with the store.

Apple Pay can also be used to pay for apps in the online App Store, and for this, you can also use the Touch ID sensor built into the Home button of iPad Air 2, iPad mini 3, and newer devices (but you can't use the tablet to pay at retail). Checking out is as easy as selecting Apple Pay from the list of options and placing your finger or thumb on the Home button.

Before you can use Apple Pay — on any device — you first need to establish your Apple Pay account.

Setting Up Apple Pay

 Setting up your iPhone for Apple Pay involves your Passbook app, which stores such things as boarding passes, movie tickets, store coupons, loyalty cards, and more. It can also store your credit and debit cards too.

To set up Apple Pay on your iPhone, follow these steps:

1. **Tap the Passbook app.**

   This launches the Passbook app.

2. **Tap the + sign next to Apple Pay in the upper-right corner.**

   This lets you add a new card. On a compatible iPad, tap Add Credit or Debit Card. Alternatively, you can also go to Settings, choose Passbook & Apple Pay, and then select Add Credit or Debit Card.

3. **If you want to use the same credit or debit card that's tied to your iTunes/App Store account, enter the card's security code.**

   As you likely know, it's located on the back of your card.

4. **To add a new credit or debit card, use your device's iSight camera (your main rear-facing camera) to capture the information on your credit and debit card or choose to enter it in manually.**

   You have to fill in additional information it might ask for, such as the security code.

5. **Your bank then verifies your information and decides if you can add your card to Apple Pay.**

   Not all banks are supported, but many are. You may be prompted to provide additional information to verify it's you — for your own security and privacy.

6. **Tap Next after your card is verified.**

   You can now start using Apple Pay at supported retailers and in the App Store. Keep in mind that the first card you add is your default payment card, but you can go to the Passbook app anytime to pay with a different card (or select a new default in Settings⇨Passbook & Apple Pay). Otherwise, you don't need to do anything. See the "Looking at the Passbook App" section later in this chapter for more on changing your default card and other options.

Whenever you use your credit or debit card at a retailer, your card number and identity, including your name, is visible to the retailer. This can cause privacy and security risks. Instead, Apple Pay uses a unique Device Account Number (DAN) for each transaction. This DAN is generated, encrypted (securely block from outsiders), and then stored in the Secure Element — a dedicated chip inside the iPhone, iPad, and Apple Watch. Apple says these numbers are never stored on Apple servers. The DAN and a dynamically generated security code are used to process your payment when purchasing something; therefore, your actual credit or debit card number is never shared by Apple with the retailer.

What happens if you lose your iPhone, iPad, or Apple Watch? Don't worry about any of them being used to make a purchase because you need your unique finger on the Touch ID sensor (Home button) or a PIN for Apple Watch. If you ever misplace your phone or tablet, use the Find My iPhone feature on the iCloud website www.icloud.com or on another iOS device to quickly put your device in Lost Mode to suspend Apple Pay or you can completely wipe your device clean of any data. Sadly, Apple Watch doesn't have a Find My Apple Watch feature.

Benefits, loyalties, and privileges

After you've attached your favorite credit and debit cards to Apple Pay and you begin shopping with your iPhone or Apple Watch, you'll notice you still benefit from all the advantages of those cards, such as loyalty rewards (points, cash back, free flights, or whatever), along with any other benefits and security privileges your card company offers.

Using Apple Pay With Your Apple Watch

Because you're wearing Apple Watch as opposed to holding it, Apple Pay on Apple Watch is even easier and faster to use at retail than an iPhone. Simply wave your Apple Watch over a contactless terminal at a supporting retailer.

Those wearing an Apple Watch can keep their phones tucked away in a purse or pocket — or even left at home if preferred — but the payment process is similar.

To pay for something with your Apple Watch, follow these steps:

1. **Step up to a contactless point-of-sale terminal.**

   Yes, this is the same one used for supported smartphones and NFC-enabled cards, such as Visa's PayWave, MasterCard's PayPass, and Amex's ExpressPay. The person behind you might not be sure what you're doing. Just smile and proceed to the next step.

2. **Double-tap the Side button on Apple Watch.**

   You're now ready to make the *digital handshake*.

3. **Hold the face up to the terminal, and within a second or two, a tone and slight vibration confirms your payment information has been successfully sent.**

   You won't need to open an Apple Pay app on the watch or anything like that. No wonder Apple calls it "Your wallet. Without a wallet."

You will, though, have to open the Apple Pay app if you want to switch cards while paying. To do that, follow these steps:

1. **Double-tap the Side button to bring up Passbook.**

   You can also say "Hey, Siri, Passbook" or press the Digital Crown button and find and tap the Passbook app. This is a similar process to paying using Apple Pay, but don't hold your watch up to the contactless terminal just yet.

2. **Swipe up or down with your fingertip or twist the Digital Crown button to browse through your cards.**

3. **Select the card you want.**

4. **Hold the Apple Watch face near the NFC reader to pay.**

   You should feel a slight vibration and hear a small chime to confirm the transaction was successfully completed.

You might start using Apple Pay with your Apple Watch quite a bit. During Apple's Spring Forward event in early March 2015, Apple CEO Tim Cook proudly confirmed that 2,500 banks as well as roughly 700,000 retail locations (and even some vending machines) now support Apple Pay. Not bad for a technology that only debuted on October 20, 2014 — and just in the United States. (Apple Pay should be available in Canada and the United Kingdom in late 2015.)

Apple Watch works with any iPhone 5 or newer, but only the iPhone 6 and newer, the latest (2014) iPads and newer, and Apple Watch can use Apple Pay. That said, you can still set up Apple Pay for Apple Watch with an iPhone 5, iPhone 5S, or iPhone 5C because the required Secure Element is in the watch (and not on the older iPhones).

Paying Without a Nearby iPhone

Apple Pay on Apple Watch is secure.

Remember, Apple Pay differs from most other mobile payment solutions because your credit or debit card number is never visible to the retailer — and thus safer to use.

When you add your card information to Apple Watch, that unique and encrypted Device Account Number (DAN) is assigned and stored on a dedicated chip inside the watch (that Secure Element technology, like with the newer iPhones and iPads).

"But wait a sec," you're thinking. "Apple Pay on iPhone requires your fingerprint on the Touch ID sensor, so how do I do that on Apple Watch?"

To enable Apple Pay on the watch, you need to create a four-digit passcode using the companion Apple Watch app on your iPhone. This passcode is used to authorize Apple Pay whenever you put the watch on your wrist. Go to My Watch⇨Settings⇨Passcode to enable and create a passcode using the virtual keyboard, as shown in Figure 10-1.

And as you might guess, those sensors on the back of the watch aren't just used for your heartbeat; they *know* whenever the watch has been taken off. And you must once again type in your secret passcode when you put the Apple Watch back on your wrist.

Clever, eh?

That way, if someone puts on your Apple Watch or tries to use it without slapping it on his or her wrist, your information is safe because the other person won't know your passcode.

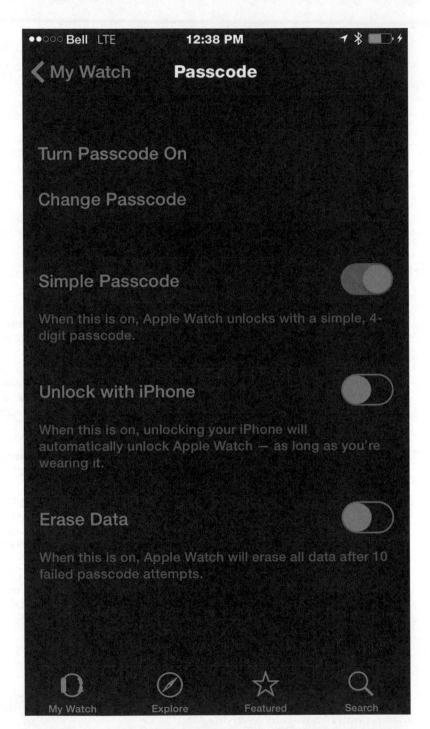

Figure 10-1: Use the virtual keyboard on your iPhone to create your four-digit passcode for your Apple Watch.

Looking at the Passbook App

Just like the app on your iOS devices — iPhone, iPad, or iPod touch — Passbook is available on Apple Watch, and it also lets you store your airline boarding passes, movie and sports tickets, coupons, loyalty cards, and much more, as shown in Figure 10-2. Think of it as a kind of digital wallet.

In other sections in this chapter, I talk about how Passbook also houses your payment cards — credit or debit — for use with Apple Pay and how to change between cards if you like, but here, I cover other things you can do with the Passbook app.

After all, accessing Passbook from your wrist is awesome — like having an airline attendant scan a QR code on your wrist while you're negotiating an important deal on your iPhone. Plus, location and time services allow Passbook to notify you about relevant information just when you need it, such as gate changes at the airport.

Introduced in iOS 6, Passbook is "a digital representation of information that might otherwise be printed on small pieces of paper or plastic," Apple says. "They let users take an action in the physical world."

Figure 10-2: Aside from buying something at retail, Passbook stores all your tickets, loyalty cards, event passes, and more.

When you download an app that supports Passbook, you have the option to add it to Passbook. You can flip through these apps — represented by virtual cards — with your fingertip to see each of the services inside Passbook and get them ready for when you need them. Or you can be notified when you step inside of a supported retailer or another location. Of if you need to know other information, such as a cancelled concert.

How to get going?

Passbook is already preinstalled on all iPhones, and if the app you download supports it, Passbook will likely ask you if that particular app can be added to your Passbook. Examples of supported apps include United Airlines, Target, Ticketmaster, Fandango, Walgreens, and Starbucks.

For example, to use the Starbucks app, follow these steps on your iPhone:

1. **Download the Starbucks app from the App Store.**

2. **Sign up for the Starbucks Rewards loyalty program or sign in if you're already a member.**

   You're prompted with this message: "Would you like to add your Starbucks card to your Passbook?"

3. **Tap Continue to add Starbucks to Passbook, as shown in Figure 10-3.**

   This message appears: "Choose your favorite stores, and your Starbucks card will appear on your lock screen when you arrive."

   Let the phone's GPS locate the nearest Starbucks and then you can select a few as favorites. When you're done, you should see the Starbucks card pop up in your Passport — with a scannable QR code and cash balance of your account. You can now open up the Passbook app — or hold out your Apple Watch — to have the screen scanned by a barista at the cash register.

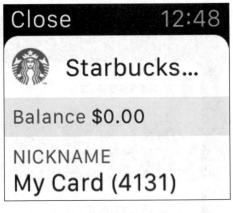

Figure 10-3: Arguably, Starbucks is one of the more popular Passbook-supported loyalty cards. This is what the Starbucks app looks like on your Apple Watch.

Using Apple Watch for Other Deals and Rewards

Apple Watch isn't just used to make purchases and offer support for loyalty cards; it can also be used in other ways to serve up a richer shopping experience.

Folding in other technologies, Apple Watch can also be used to customize the store experience to suit individual preferences. For example, stores equipped with Apple's iBeacon location-based technology (developer.apple.com/ibeacon) could identify you from your Apple Watch (and/or nearby iPhone) and welcome you, reward you with points for stepping into a store, notify you about deals, and give personalized suggestions based on previous interests.

Of course, these are things you have to opt into. That is, you must give the store permission first in its downloadable app.

Imagine stepping into a retailer and seeing what you need to know on the Apple Watch screen. It's still early days, but the technology is there.

Just ask Cyriac Roeding, the celebrated entrepreneur, investor, and cofounder/ CEO of shopkick, an app that helps you find deals and earn rewards.

"While it's still a little early, smartwatches like Apple Watch are a next, natural step in the evolution of the shopping experience," believes Roeding, whose shopkick app is the most widely used shopping app at retail stores in the United States, according to Nielsen, with approximately 10 million users (as of May 2015).

Roeding says shopkick's Apple Watch app will offer much of the same experience as the smartphone app "but without you having to take out your phone." When you walk into one of the 10,000 stores with shopkick's shopBeacon transmitters — built upon Apple's location-based iBeacon technology — you'll be welcomed by name, rewarded with redeemable *kicks* (points) for walking in the door, and notified of curated deals based on your previous shopping habits. See Figure 10-4 for an example of shopkick's technology (courtesy of shopkick).

Figure 10-4: A look at shopkick's shopBeacon transmitter on the wall of a retailer.

"Just like with smartphones, our goal for Apple Watch will be to turn *a* store you walk into [into] *your* store. We'll show you what you need on the watch screen — call it 'mini shopkick' — but if there's more info you'll need you'll be directed to open the app on your iPhone," says Roeding.

shopBeacon's location technology, which uses ultrasound and Bluetooth low energy (BLE), does not collect any information about you, assures Roeding, because it only sends out information instead of collecting data.

Part IV
More Apple Watch Tips and Tricks

Visit www.dummies.com for more great *Dummies* content online.

In this part . . .

✔ Learn how to download apps to your Apple Watch as well as how to establish and modify settings in the companion Apple Watch app on your iPhone.

✔ Customize your Apple Watch by adding third-party apps, including your favorite iPhone apps, such as ESPN, Twitter, TripAdvisor, NPR One, and Fandango.

✔ Discover how to turn your Apple Watch into a camera, including storing and viewing photos from your iPhone, as well as a remote control for using the camera on your iPhone.

✔ Enhance your Apple Watch experience by downloading gaming apps, including such iPhone favorites as Trivia Crack and Best Fiends.

11

App It Up: Customizing Apple Watch With Awesome Apps and More

*N*o two people are exactly alike, so why should our devices have the same apps installed?

Just like it's fun to customize a smartphone or tablet screen with all kinds of hand-picked apps — short for "applications," which is just a more trendy way to say "software" or "programs" — Apple Watch supports many thousands of third-party (non-Apple) apps.

The App Store for Apple Watch is already jammed with apps designed for your sleek wearable, including many familiar apps (perhaps based on its iPhone or iPad brethren) and completely new apps looking to dominate this new screen in your life. In most cases, they're free to download (or close to it), and you're sure to find something that resonates with you.

Bottom line: We're all individuals who have different tastes, priorities, and interests.

This chapter looks at how to choose and install Apple Watch apps, sync them over to the watch, and manage them from your Home screen. I take you through the companion Apple Watch app for iPhone and how to tweak settings and personalization options. Toward the end of this chapter, I also suggest several stellar apps you might want to consider for your watch. (See Chapter 12 for a brief discussion about gaming apps for your Apple Watch.).

Downloading Apps for Apple Watch

While Watch OS is a brand-new platform, expect the development community to fully embrace it right out of the gate.

If the incredible success of Apple's App Store — for iOS devices (iPhone, iPad, and iPod touch) and OS X (Mac) computers — is any indication, developers will want to capitalize on Apple Watch. Imagine the millions of customers who are wearing this new gadget on their wrists and the different ways they're going to want to customize that experience with apps.

In case you weren't aware, developers make 70 percent on paid apps, with the remaining 30 percent going to Apple. Thus, an opportunity exists to make some serious cash by creating a must-have app for Apple Watch.

"The more you wear Apple Watch, the more you'll realize just how personal a device it is," says Apple on its website. "Because with so many different apps available, you can choose the ones that are most relevant to you and create a customized experience.

"There are already apps for airlines, department stores, social networks and more that take advantage of the unique opportunities the wrist brings. And with new apps being built for Apple Watch every day, this is just the beginning," adds Apple.

How does one go about downloading apps?

From the App Store — but not the same App Store as the one on your iPhone, iPad, iPod touch, or Mac nor can you download apps for Apple Watch through iTunes on a Windows PC or Mac. It's a separate store solely dedicated to Apple Watch, as shown in Figure 11-1.

And no, you can't download apps on the watch itself. But the Apple Watch App Store *is* built into the Apple Watch app on your iPhone.

To use the Apple Watch App Store on your iPhone, follow these steps:

1. **On your iPhone, tap the Apple Watch app.**

   The black icon with a silver Apple Watch is preinstalled with the update for iOS 8.2 — and no, you can't delete it from your iPhone (even if you don't have an Apple Watch). Tapping the app launches the App Store for Apple Watch.

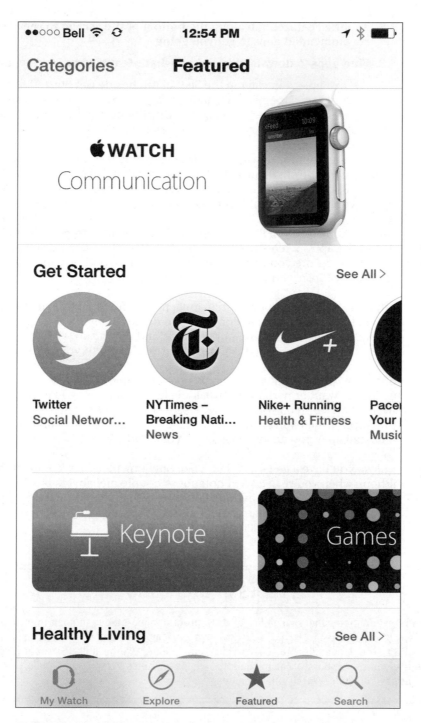

Figure 11-1: A look at the App Store for Apple Watch, which is part of the iPhone app for Apple Watch.

2. **Tap the Featured tab along the bottom of the screen to see some recommended apps to get you going.**

3. **Find apps to download based on what's featured or by category.**

   For example, you can tap the See All tab beside Get Started to open up a list of popular apps. Alternatively, tap the Search tab — as shown in Figure 11-2 — in the lower right of the iPhone screen if you'd prefer to look for something by keyword instead of browsing.

Many of the Apple Watch apps are free, and most require a nearby iPhone to get the most from them. In fact, remember that Apple Watch apps always have a companion app for iPhone; therefore, you need to have enough storage on your iPhone — not just on the watch.

For any App Store you like to shop at, it's a good idea to read the full description of the app and check out the screenshots before you download to ensure it's for you before you waste your time, data, and, perhaps, money. Also, read reviews by those who've already used the app.

After you download Apple Watch apps, they automatically sync to your watch. In other words, you don't need to do anything to copy apps over to the watch. The moment the Apple Watch and iPhone are synced over Wi-Fi or Bluetooth, whatever you downloaded is transferred to your wrist.

But if you want to manage the apps on your Apple Watch, including ones you no longer want or perhaps to tweak the layout of them, you need to use the Apple Watch app on your iPhone. As covered in this chapter, simply launch the Apple Watch app on your iPhone and then tap My Watch, where you can uninstall apps you no longer want on your Apple Watch.

Unless you have a generous data plan, only download large apps on your iPhone when you're in a Wi-Fi hotspot. A couple megabytes is fine if you're using cellular data, but anything larger than that should be done using wireless broadband. Some games can be a couple gigabytes in size (1 gigabyte is roughly 1,000 megabytes).

Tools of the trade

Apple first announced the availability of its WatchKit (developer.apple.com/watchkit) on November 18, 2014. This software gives developers a set of tools to create apps for Apple Watch and includes programming guides, human interface guidelines, templates, and more. Starting in late 2015, developers will be able to create fully native apps for Apple Watch, says Apple.

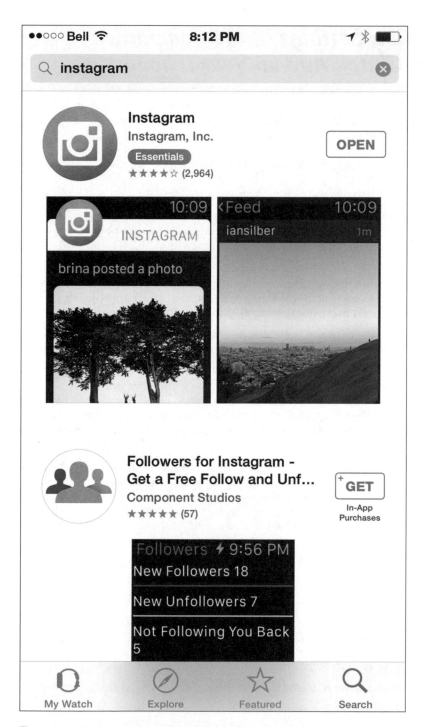

Figure 11-2: Use keywords, such as "instagram," to find new content for your Apple Watch.

Adjusting Settings in the Companion Apple Watch App on Your iPhone

Instead of tapping on the App Store tab in the lower right of the Apple Watch app on iPhone — where you download Apple Watch apps — tap the My Watch tab in the lower left to open up the settings and personalization options for the watch.

From within My Watch, you can perform the following actions:

✔ Change the orange **App Layout** of the apps on your Apple Watch's Home screen.

✔ The blue **Apple Watch** tells you which model you have, such as 42mm Case - Aluminum. You can unpair Apple Watch from the iPhone from here too.

✔ Review and change which apps you want Notifications and Glances for in their respective **Notifications** app (red) and **Glances** app (blue). You can make changes to all your installed apps.

✔ Adjust brightness and text size for the watch in the blue-and-white **Brightness & Text Size** section. As shown in Figure 11-3, use the slider to adjust each setting and choose to bold text or not.

✔ Enable or disable sounds and vibrations in the red-and-white **Sounds & Haptics** area (also shown in Figure 11-3). You should have options for Alert Volume, Mute, Cover to Mute (covering your watch with your hand to mute it), Haptic Strength, and Prominent Haptic for more pronounced vibrations.

✔ The purple **Do Not Disturb** tab turns off all alerts, sounds, and haptics to the watch, while the orange **Airplane Mode** disables the wireless connection between Apple Watch and the iPhone. When enabled, the **Mirror iPhone** option automatically turns off Apple Watch's wireless radios whenever you do the same on the iPhone.

✔ You should also find options for **Passcode** (enable a passcode on Apple Watch and select the four-digit code); **Health** (your birth date, sex, height, and weight for the purposes of estimating your calories burned); and **General**.

Under General options for Apple Watch, you should find the following information:

✔ **About:** Software version installed and other information.

✔ **Software Update:** To look for and download the latest Watch OS update.

✔ **Automatic Downloads:** For Watch OS and app updates.

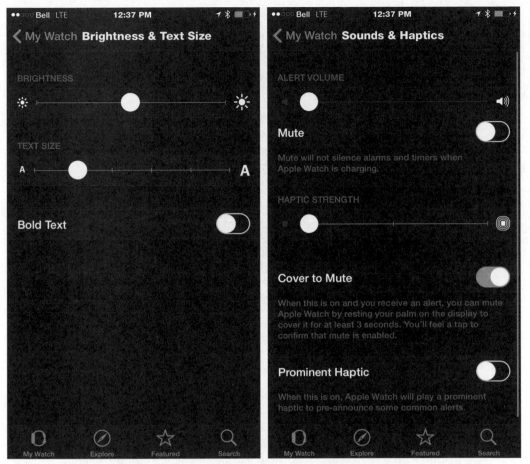

Figure 11-3: Use your fingertip to adjust settings for brightness, text size, sounds, and haptics.

- ✔ **Watch Orientation:** Left or right wrist and whether the Digital Crown button is on the left or right side. You have the ability to change this, as shown in Figure 11-4.

- ✔ **Accessibility:** Options/aids for seeing and hearing impaired and more.

- ✔ **Language & Region:** Choose the System Languages, Region, and Calendar type (which by default is Gregorian).

- ✔ **Apple ID:** The account you're signed in to.

- ✔ **Enable Handoff:** When this is on, your iPhone picks up where you left off with supported apps on your Apple Watch.

- ✔ **Wrist Detection:** When this is on, Apple Watch automatically shows you the time and latest alerts when you raise your wrist.

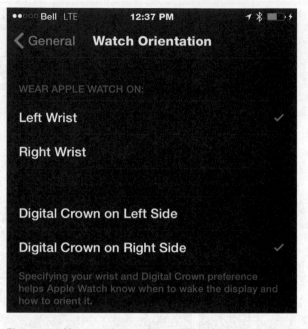

Figure 11-4: You can change the watch's orientation from left wrist (default) to right and which side the Digital Crown button is on.

Accessibility options

Those living with visual or aural impairments can take advantage of a number of accessibility options on Apple Watch. Just as Apple has done with its iOS and OS X products (and the Safari web browser), Apple's first smartwatch provides several features you can enable in the Accessibility area of the Apple Watch app on your iPhone, as shown in Figure 11-5. More details are available at Apple's website for these options (www.apple.com/accessibility/watch), but the following provides a quick summary:

- ✔ Visually impaired users can enable **VoiceOver**, a screen reader available in one of 14 languages.

- ✔ Enlarge the Apple Watch fonts in **Font Adjustment** (ideal for the Mail, Messages, and Settings apps), add **Bold Text**, and opt for the **Extra Large Watch Face** option with bigger numbers to read.

- ✔ Other visual tweaks include **Zoom** (magnification), **Grayscale** (no color), **Reduce Transparency** (increases contrast), **On/Off Labels** (easier to see if setting is on or off), and **Reduce Motion** (the Home screen is easier to navigate).

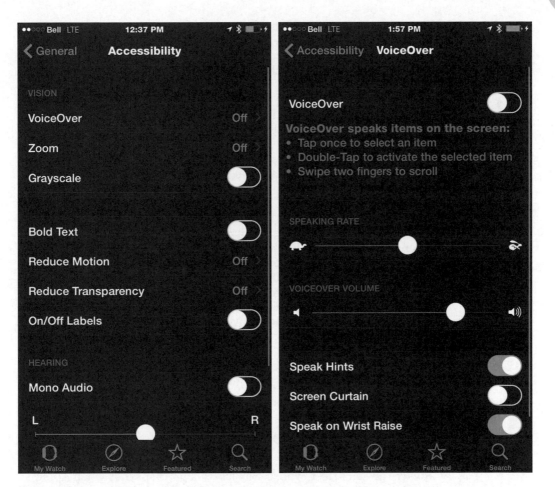

Figure 11-5: You can adjust a number of accessibility options for Apple Watch, as shown in the Apple Watch app for iPhone.

✔ For those with impaired hearing, Apple Watch lets you enable **Mono Audio** (sending both audio channels to both ears and letting you adjust balance for greater volume in one ear or another).

✔ Apple Watch's Taptic Engine can be enhanced with **Prominent Haptic**, a setting that gives a slightly more noticeable vibration and "preannouncement" for some alerts, such as calendar appointments, messages, phone calls, and more. A *preannouncement* means the watch sends you an additional haptic vibration before the main one.

✔ The **Friends** ring lets you choose which friends to see when you press the Side button. You can add up to 12 of your contacts to the Friends screen — each assigned a color — and you can call, send a message, or use Digital Touch to reach out. See Chapter 5 for more on the Friends ring.

REMEMBER

You can also adjust some Accessibility options on Apple Watch itself by triple-tapping the Digital Crown button.

Of course, multiple options and settings can be explored in each of the first-party apps installed on Apple Watch: Activity, Calendar, Clock, Mail, Maps, Messages, Music, Passbook & Apple Pay, Phone, Photos, Reminders, Stocks, Weather, and Workout. Some examples of what you can change include:

✔ **Clock:** You can select 12- or 24-hour (military) time; Push Alerts from iPhone (if enabled, Apple Watch lets you know about iPhone alerts); Notifications Indication (if enabled, a red dot appears at the top of the watch face when you have unread Notifications); Monogram (choose a one- to four-letter monogram to appear as a monogram complication on the Color watch face); and City Abbreviations (specifying different acronyms for the default ones provided for your chosen cities for the world clock complications).

✔ **Activity:** You can choose to turn on or off Stand Reminders (notified 50 minutes into an hour of inactivity); Progress Updates (set a time interval to receive an update on your Activity progress, such as every five hours); Goal Completions (on or off); Achievements (on or off); and Weekly Summary (on or off — received every Monday).

✔ **Messages:** You can see all the default replies or change them to anything you like.

✔ **Music:** You can select Synced Playlist (this playlist syncs when Apple Watch is on its charger) and Playlist Limit (such as changing it from 2 gigabytes to 1 GB).

Twenty Recommended Third-Party Apple Watch Apps

In Chapter 3, we looked at all the default apps preinstalled on Apple Watch — you know, the ones Apple put there and you can't remove (which understandably frustrates a number of people) — but I want to share a number of optional but recommended and free third-party apps you can download from the Apple Watch App Store.

All of them take advantage of Apple Watch's features. Because I reserve games for Chapter 12, these 20 apps are tied more to information, travel, automotive, productivity, social media, fitness, shopping, and some entertainment.

Mint

The Apple Watch app for this popular finance tool lets you view your monthly spending goals at a glance as well as track your progress toward meeting them. And for those trying to stick to a budget, you can choose to receive weekly alerts with insight on how well you're doing (or not).

ESPN

One of the most popular sports apps for iPhone is now available for Apple Watch. Select which sports matter to you — such as baseball, football, basketball, hockey, golf, or tennis (or all the above) — and stay up to date with breaking sports news, real-time scores, and more, as shown in Figure 11-6.

Figure 11-6: The ESPN app should be a good fit for Apple Watch–wearing sports fans.

Target

As one of the first retailers to support Apple Watch, Target has an app that lets you build and view a shopping list on your watch so you can glance down to see what items you need — even if your phone is tucked away in your purse or pocket. When you enter a store, the Target app also tells you where to find the items you're looking for.

OneDrive

While once bitter rivals, Microsoft has embraced Apple's iOS platform — and now the Watch OS too. Based on Microsoft's OneDrive cloud service, this Apple Watch app lets users see their stored photos on their wrist — even when an iPhone isn't nearby.

SPG

As shown in Figure 11-7, one of the cooler apps is from Starwood Hotels & Resorts, which lets you unlock your hotel door by waving your Apple Watch at the sensor. A room key isn't required. The official SPG (Starwood Preferred Guest) app can also provide directions to your hotel, check you in, show your Starpoints balance, and more.

Figure 11-7: The SPG app lets you open up hotel doors in select Starwood hotels.

Twitter

See your Twitter feeds right on your wrist. And because they're 140 characters or less, tweets fit perfectly on Apple Watch's small screen. Feel a gentle tap whenever new tweets are posted, plus you can retweet and favorite tweets from your Apple Watch. If you want to say something to the Twitterverse, compose it via dictation. Just tap the square compose icon — in the center of the screen — and say what you'd like to tweet.

OpenTable

Hungry? The OpenTable app now supports Apple Watch, which lets you see information about your upcoming dinner reservations by simply looking down at your wrist. The app can also help guide you to the restaurant with turn-by-turn directions.

Evernote

A popular productivity tool, Evernote for Apple Watch lets you view your stored notes, dictate a new one, set reminders, and search by keyword if you're looking for something in particular. Because Evernote stores your notes in the cloud, you can view your dictated notes in other Evernote apps — perhaps on a smartphone, tablet, or laptop.

American Airlines

How do you know when it's time to leave for the airport? Or if your flight has been delayed, cancelled, or changed gates? American Airlines (AA) has an Apple Watch app that can alert you to any and all of these things. The AA app also lets you check in for your flight, view a map with your estimated time of arrival, view baggage claim and connection details, and more, as shown in Figure 11-8.

BMW i Remote

Own an electric BMW i vehicle? The official Apple Watch app lets you remotely check on the charge status or it can notify you when your car has been fully charged and is ready to go. This smartwatch app also lets you check your miles (to prevent "range anxiety"), see door-lock status, get service reminders, and view your cabin temperature.

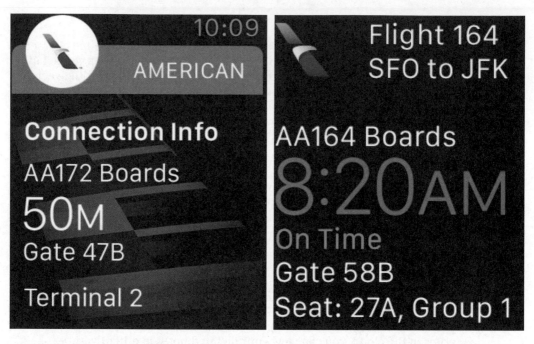

Figure 11-8: The American Airlines app notifies you of changes to your flight and more.

CNN

News junkies, rejoice! The official CNN app for Apple Watch gives you the information you need wherever life takes you. Select to receive breaking news and developing stories based on 12 categories of interest — such as Top Stories, U.S., World, Politics, Health, Entertainment, Sports, and Technology — plus your watch can even launch CNN TV live on your iPhone.

eBay

The world's largest marketplace is now a tap away. eBay on Apple Watch helps you keep up with the auctions you're watching — whether you're bidding on something or selling merchandise. The app conveniently lets you send and receive alerts without having to fumble through your phone, tablet, or personal computer.

Citymapper

If you rely on public transit, the Citymapper app for Apple Watch always shows you the best bus and train routes based on your location and where you want to go. You should see step-by-step instructions, including a list of the next three arrival times for your mode of transportation so you can decide when to leave, and you should feel a vibration on your wrist when it's time to get off at your stop. See Figure 11-9 for a look at the Citymapper app.

TripAdvisor

Find that hidden gem of a restaurant on your next trip. Unearth dozens of things to do while discovering a new town. Everything that makes TripAdvisor the perfect travel companion is now on your Apple Watch. Get instant information on hundreds of nearby restaurants, sights, and tourist destinations.

NPR One

Fans of NPR can make their favorite station even more personal. The NPR One app shows you relevant news and curated stories based on your interests, along with access to your playlist (on your iPhone), and you can search for specific shows by using dictation and control basic playback functions with your fingertip.

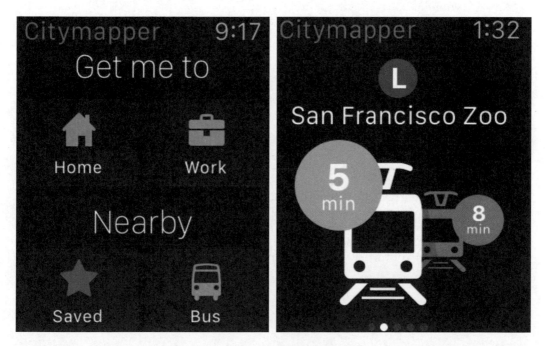

Figure 11-9: Ideal for those who take public transit, the Citymapper app for Apple Watch shows you relevant information.

Fandango

The popular movie ticketing app is now on your wrist. After you've purchased tickets to a flick, the Apple Watch app can display the movie time and theater location, phone number, and other information you might need.

Shazam

It's happened to all of us: You hear a song you like but have no idea who sings it (and, of course, the DJ doesn't say the name either). Or you hear an amazing song in a commercial and are equally stumped. The Shazam app for Apple Watch can be used to listen to what's playing, and within a second or two, your watch displays the name of the song, the artist, and even the lyrics.

PayByPhone Parking

The PayByPhone Parking app on Apple Watch can be used to pay the meter, check on the time remaining, and deliver an alert ten minutes before the meter expires. If you're not done with your errands, your watch lets you add more time to the meter without your having to go back to your car.

Sky Guide

Watch the skies! And your wrist. As shown in Figure 11-10, the Sky Guide app for Apple Watch is great for armchair astronomers. Receive alerts about upcoming celestial events — such as meteor shows and eclipses — and it even alerts you when the International Space Station is about to fly over your location.

Lutron Caséta

Your smartwatch can control your smarthome. The Lutron Caséta app for Apple Watch lets you control the lights in your home — even when you're not there. (Make it look like you're home when you're on vacation.) Or on the flipside, if you accidentally leave the lights on when you leave, you can get an alert on your wrist to turn them off.

Figure 11-10: The Sky Guide app is out of this world. Read about astronomical events and receive alerts about them too.

12

Extra! Extra! Having Fun With Apple Watch

*Y*ou didn't think Apple Watch was just for information, communication, and navigation, did you?

This mobile companion of yours is also ideal for playing around. In Chapter 5, I looked at how to send animated emojis and digital sketches to people. And Chapter 9 covered music playback and how to control Apple TV and iTunes playlists from your wrist.

But your watch can do much more in the fun department.

Granted, Apple doesn't seem to advertise these nonessential applications as much as customizing watch faces, sending messages, or calculating your physical activity, but you can indeed enjoy some downtime with Apple Watch, including many playable games already available in the App Store for Apple Watch.

You can also look at photos of people, pets, and places on your Apple Watch — anytime and anywhere. Perhaps you ran into someone who asked how old your daughter is. Now you can show that person her smiling face. Or maybe you want to glance down to see old friends when a song on the radio brings back camp memories. If you're feeling like you need a vacation, call up photos of last year's trip to Jamaica so you can see the white sand and blue water (and then call your travel agent!).

Speaking of photos, Apple Watch can let you access your iPhone's camera to snap the shutter button wirelessly, which is ideal for selfies and group shots. This is available through the Camera Remote app.

Using the Photos App for Apple Watch

Okay, so Apple Watch doesn't have the biggest screen in your life, but it *is* always on your wrist; therefore, it's a conveniently placed digital photo frame.

One of the built-in apps is Photos, which is similar to the photo gallery app on your iPhone, iPod touch, or iPad.

To use the Photos app on your Apple Watch, follow these steps:

1. **Tap the Digital Crown button to go to the Home screen.**

2. **Tap the Photos app.**

   If you prefer, raise your wrist and say "Hey, Siri, Photos." Either action launches the Photos app, which shows you thumbnails of photos stored on your phone (or watch).

3. **Twist the Digital Crown button to zoom in and out on individual images.**

   Twisting the Digital Crown away from you zooms out to see more photos, which makes the thumbnails smaller, while twisting toward you zooms into a photo.

4. **Zoom in until a photo takes up the entire watch face.**

   Now you can swipe left and right to browse through your photos one at a time. The photos are in the same order as they are on your iPhone's Photos app, including any albums you've created. Figure 12-1 shows a photo full screen on Apple Watch.

   Why doesn't Apple Watch allow you to pinch and zoom? Your finger and thumb would cover up your photos. The Digital Crown button works better.

5. **Twist the Digital Crown button to zoom out to see more photos or tap the Digital Crown button to exit the Photos app and return to the Home screen.**

   Speaking of photos, don't forget Apple Watch can show you images that are embedded/attached to Messages and Mail (email). You should see images just below the text in a given message. Twist the Digital Crown button to see the accompanying photo(s) near the bottom of the screen. Too bad you can't send a photo to someone from Apple Watch. For that, you need to use your iPhone.

Figure 12-1: Swipe your finger left or right to scroll through all your photos. Hey, that's the author of *Apple Watch For Dummies* and his better half!

A fast way to see photos of people you care about it to press the Side button on Apple Watch, which brings up your Friends ring. You can twist the Digital Crown button to see up to 12 faces of people you care about.

How to Copy Photos to Apple Watch

For most tasks, Apple Watch requires a nearby iPhone. The two devices are wirelessly tethered via Bluetooth and Wi-Fi, but you can sync some files to Apple Watch — just in case your iPhone isn't nearby.

Chapter 9 talks about syncing music to the watch — perhaps if you want to go for a jog around the neighborhood without your phone and you own a Bluetooth headset — but here, I cover transferring photos over to your watch.

I'm not exactly sure *why* you'd want to copy photos to your watch — unless you really think you're going to want to see some pictures when your iPhone isn't nearby. Having music on the watch makes more sense — per my jogging scenario — but those who want to take advantage of this feature must first enable it on the Apple Watch app on iPhone.

As shown in Figures 12-2 and 12-3, you've got some options in the Photos area of the Apple Watch app on iPhone:

- **Synced Album:** Select which iPhone-stored photos are viewable on Apple Watch — even when you don't have your iPhone with you. By default, it's your Favorites album, but you can also choose another one, such as Camera Roll. Or select None.

- **Photos Limit:** Select the photo storage limit on your Apple Watch. Although this limit is measured in megabytes (MB), you can raise or lower the number, but 15 MB is the default number, which translates to 100 photos. Lowering it to 5 MB only loads 25 photos. You can raise it to 40 MB (250 photos) or a maximum of 75 MB (500 photos).

Interestingly, you can also copy up to 2 gigabytes of music to Apple Watch, which translates to roughly 500 songs. Therefore, you can store up to 500 photos and up to 500 tunes. You can't go over this maximum for photos and music.

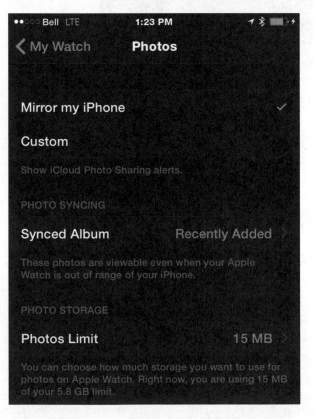

Figure 12-2: Select which photos you want synced to Apple Watch (if any).

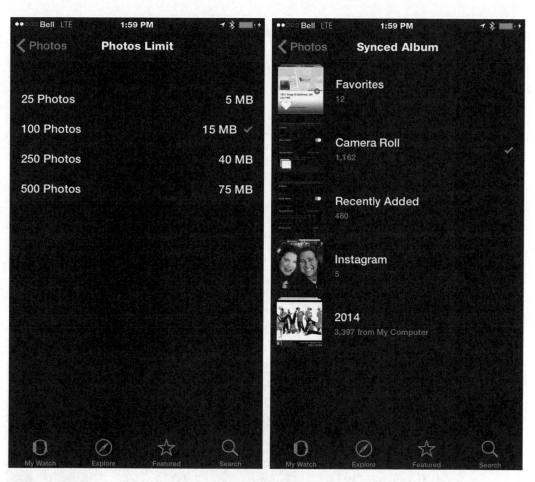

Figure 12-3: Select how many photos you'd like to sync (by size or number of files) and from which album.

Pop goes the culture

Speaking of photos, among the first celebrities seen wearing Apple Watch — even before it went on sale April 24, 2015 — were pop star Katy Perry and Canadian rapper Drake (both of whom were donning a yellow gold watch with a red leather band) as well as "Happy" singer/ songwriter Pharrell (with white leather band). Being a celeb has its perks!

Discovering the Camera Remote App

Did you know you can use Apple Watch as a viewfinder for your iPhone's iSight (rear-facing) camera? You can see a preview of your photo before you take it, set the camera timer on your watch, or just take the photo.

The Camera Remote app might be ideal for those who want to get in the picture but don't want to press the iPhone's shutter button (on the screen or a button along the side of the phone). It can be awkward to hold the camera and take a selfie at the same time or worse — risk dropping your iPhone and breaking the glass. Or you can use one of those selfie sticks too.

To use the Camera Remote app on your Apple Watch, follow these steps:

1. **Tap the Digital Crown button to go to the Home screen.**

2. **Tap the Camera Remote app.**

   Alternatively, you can lift your wrist and say "Hey, Siri, Camera Remote." Either action launches the Camera Remote app. You should then see a preview of your iPhone's iSight camera.

3. **Frame up your shot by getting your subjects huddled together or centering a landscape photo or whatever, as shown in Figure 12-4.**

   Consider Apple Watch your live viewfinder for the iPhone you're holding (or one you've placed on a tripod).

4. **If you want to take a photo, press the white shutter button in the center of the watch — just below the preview window.**

   This instantly snaps the picture and adds a thumbnail to the bottom left of your Apple Watch's screen. You can tap this thumbnail if you'd like to see the photo full screen.

Figure 12-4: No broccoli in the teeth? As you can see here, you can take a selfie or a group shot with friends.

5. **If you want to use the timer, tap where it says 3s (3 seconds). Tap the white shutter button — shown in Figure 12-5 — and you should see a countdown on the screen before the photo is taken.**

   Review what you took, and if you like it, press the Digital Crown button to return to your Home screen. Don't bother pressing the white shutter button if you don't like what you see. Frame up a different shot and then press the white button.

Figure 12-5: Whether you use the timer or not, tap the large white shutter button to snap a picture by using your iPhone's iSight camera. It counts down from 3 to 1.

Camera-less smartwatch — for now

While Apple Watch can serve as a viewfinder for your iPhone's camera, letting you snap pictures wirelessly and even set the self-timer, it doesn't have its own built-in camera like some other smartwatches have. Shoppers should remember this if it's an important feature to you. Perhaps Apple will add it to future models?

Examining a Batch of Apple Watch Games

When smartphones started to take off in the early part of the 21st century — including iPhone's high-profile debut in 2007 — many video game purists said the screen was simply too small to provide a gratifying interactive entertainment experience. Why would people want to squint to play a game on a (then) 3.5-inch screen when they have a 14-inch laptop, 23-inch desktop, and 60-inch flat-panel TV at home? And don't you need a game controller with real buttons as opposed to finger taps, swipes, and flicks on a small screen?

But then came along a handful of stellar games that proved the naysayers wrong: Angry Birds, Temple Run, Flappy Bird, Subway Surfers, Cut the Rope, Candy Crush Saga, Fruit Ninja, Words With Friends, and Jetpack Joyride — to name just a few.

Gaming on a smartphone is not only convenient — because we don't go anywhere without these devices — but the App Store offers a ton of games, with most downloadable games costing just $0.99 cents — if anything at all.

Whether Apple Watch will be a viable gaming platform is still up for debate, and developers have a few obstacles to overcome — a tiny screen, limited user interface, and questionable battery life — but where there's a will, there's a way — and an app for that! Gamers love to play anywhere, anytime, and on any device, so "time" will tell whether the wrist will be the new place to game.

That hasn't stopped a number of game developers from creating digital diversions on Apple Watch — many of which were announced even before the watch became available in spring 2015.

The following is a look at a half-dozen games. Remember, to find and download these games and other apps, open the Apple Watch app on your iPhone and then tap the App Store tab in the lower-right corner of the screen.

Watch This Homerun

From Atlanta-based Eyes Wide Games comes the first of many sports games. Watch This Homerun is a watch-sized baseball experience, delivering bite-sized (10- to 15-second) game experiences. The game has you touch the screen at the right time to whack baseballs — be they fastballs, curveballs, or changeups — into the bleachers, with inaccurate taps sending you back to the bench.

The game's companion iPhone app tracks competitive leaderboards, achievements, and personal stats against friends and the rest of the community.

Future one-touch sports games include football, basketball, soccer, and boxing, says the developer. See Figure 12-6 for a look at Watch This Homerun.

Figure 12-6: Knock a baseball into the stands with Watch This Homerun.

Trivia Crack

One of 2015's most downloaded iPhone games is also available for Apple Watch. Trivia Crack (as shown in Figure 12-7) lets you play rounds of pop culture trivia — without ever taking your iPhone out of your pocket. Animated characters guide you in defeating all your opponents while you answer millions of questions submitted by users from around the world. Questions appear on the watch's screen, and you can answer them right on the watch; after an opponent answers and it's your turn, you're notified from your watch and can continue playing from there. Example: What's Muhammad Ali's real name? Rocky Balboa, Rocky Marciano, Anderson Silva, or Cassius Clay (correct answer).

Runeblade

Gamers looking for a richer gaming experience might consider Runeblade, a fantasy adventure RPG (role-playing game) that's simple enough for anyone to pick up and play but offers far more depth for players looking for a deeper experience, says Everywear Games. The company's first Apple Watch title increases in depth and complexity over days, weeks, and months

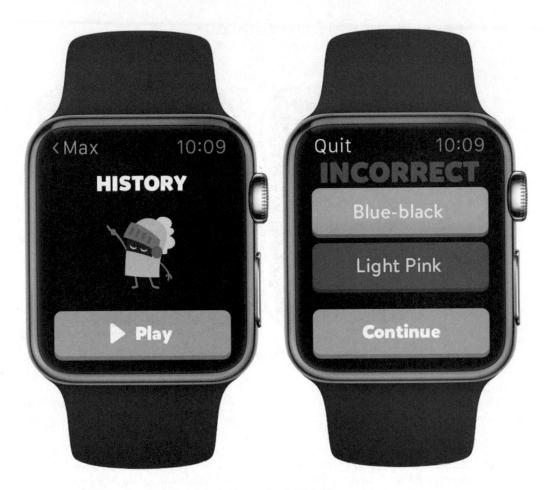

Figure 12-7: This is what Trivia Crack looks like on Apple Watch's screen.

of gameplay, although games are designed to be played in 5- to 15-second sessions. As shown in Figure 12-8, the game stars you as a High Priestess of the War Mages — challenged with stopping an ancient menace from consuming the realm as you use might and magic to defeat mystical creatures, unlock new spells and abilities, and level up to grow stronger over time.

Best Fiends

If you like such matching games as Candy Crush Saga, Apple Watch owners might enjoy tapping through Best Fiends — one of the first mobile games for the platform and based on the popular iOS version. In the single-player

Figure 12-8: Screenshots from Runeblade by Everywear Games.

puzzle game from developer Seriously, players explore the lands of Minutia, collect treasures, and battle the malevolent Slugs of Mount Boom (such as the one seen in Figure 12-9). What's more, players earn rewards that can be applied to their Best Fiends game on their iPhone — used toward leveling up characters, unlocking new powers, and defeating enemies. In the iOS version, players drag a finger up, down, and diagonally to match identical items on an obstacle-laden game board.

Snappy Word

Australian developer Right Pedal has released Snappy Word, a word game that places four random letter tiles on the watch face. By tapping the letters in order to create words, your goal is to see how many words you can create in 30 seconds. For example, "E," "M," "S" and "A" can create such words as

Figure 12-9: Best Fiends (not Best Friends) is a popular matching puzzle game that's now playable on Apple Watch.

"same," "mesa," and "as." Also playable on iPhone, iPad or iPod, this Apple Watch game (as shown in Figure 12-10) includes a real-time player-versus-player mode or you can compete against others through the Game Center leaderboard. Snappy Word's dictionary is said to be made up of nearly 4,000 words.

Watch Quest

Even before Apple Watch debuted in the spring of 2015, buzz amassed in the gaming world over an adventure title called Watch Quest. Players first choose characters on the companion app for iPhone, equip them with gear, and then have them embark on a quest on Apple Watch — filled with engaging in combat, solving puzzles, and hunting treasure. Starring a male or female protagonist, this colorful game includes passive play — slower-paced and easier quests — and more difficult active play, including battling

Figure 12-10: Snappy Word — a word game from Aussie developer Right Pedal — forces you to be quick about creating words.

monsters (as shown in Figure 12-11) and foraging for items. Watch Quest is free to download and comes with one training campaign, but you have to pay for additional quests and characters from within the iPhone app.

Spy_Watch

One of the more intriguing offerings sneaking onto Apple Watch is from UK-based indie developer Bossa Studios — best known for Surgeon Simulator and I Am Bread.

Figure 12-11: Fans of epic quests might enjoy this Apple Watch–supported adventure: Watch Quest.

In Spy_Watch, as shown in Figure 12-12, you're the head of a spy agency that's seen better days. To turn the agency around, you must train spies, send them on secret missions, and earn money to improve their abilities.

According to the developer, this ambitious Apple Watch game centers around short bursts of real-time alerts between you and your agent in the field, which take place in two- to five-second rounds. As the agency head, you need to make strategic decisions on the fly that will ultimately affect the success of the missions — be they related to time, resources, or locations. No guarantees you'll look as suave as James Bond while tapping on your wrist.

Figure 12-12: A stealthy spy game called Spy_Watch is one of the launch titles for Apple Watch.

Part V
The Part of Ten

In this part . . .

✔ Discover the top ten things you should try with your Apple
  Watch as soon as you've taken it from its box and charged it
  up. These include turning your Apple Watch into a hotel key,
  sending personalized sketches to friends and family with Digital
  Touch, and, of course, learning more ways Siri can help you in
  your day-to-day life. You can also quickly learn how to play
  music on your Apple Watch, establish your fitness goals, and
  set up Apple Pay.

13

Ten Cool Things to Do
With Your Apple Watch

In This Chapter

▶ Covering ten must-try features of Apple Watch

▶ Diving deeper with additional tips and tricks

▶ Impressing your friends with your new wrist-mounted gadget

*I*f you've spent some time flipping through this book — and thank you by the way — you've no doubt soaked up a lot of what Apple's "most personal device ... ever" can do.

Apple Watch has hundreds of use-case scenarios — many of which are provided by Apple and its built-in features — while third-party apps extend the functionality of this smartwatch even further (as evidenced in Chapters 11 and 12).

But if you're like most people, you won't have time to go over *everything* Apple Watch has to offer. As I mentioned earlier in this book, it's estimated we only use about 10 percent of what our gadgets can do — until someone shows you what you're missing.

As the author of *Siri For Dummies*, I always love that "a-ha!" moment when I teach people a Siri tip or trick they had no idea about. It's even more gratifying when they tell me at a later time that what I showed them is something they've grown to rely on in their day-to-day lives.

This brings us to this final chapter of *Apple Watch For Dummies*, where I isolate ten must-try features of Apple Watch. Consider it a purely subjective list of my favorite things about the device. Perhaps you don't know where to start or want to know how to best showcase your new gadget to friends and family. Or maybe you just want a refresher on a handful of the most useful features of Apple Watch — all in one chapter — instead of picking and choosing the individual tasks from across a couple hundred pages?

Thus, the following are my top ten features of Apple Watch and how to enable them. I also mention where in this book you can learn more about each one.

Activity

Many smartwatches and fitness bands can report on your performance while working out, but Apple Watch is always calculating what you're doing — or not doing.

The innovative Activity app and its three rings — for Move, Exercise, and Stand — does a stellar job of giving you an idea of your overall physical activity.

Press the Digital Crown button or lift your wrist and say "Hey, Siri, Activity" and then take a gander at your progress:

- The reddish-pink **Move** ring shows how many calories you've burned by moving around during the day.

- The lime-green **Exercise** ring is for minutes of brisk or intense activity you've completed that day.

- The baby-blue **Stand** ring gives you a visual indication of how often you've stood up after sitting or reclining.

Your goal is to complete each ring each day. The more solid each ring is, the better you're doing. Plus, you can swipe around inside the app for a numerical look at your performance.

You can also change your goals per day — an example is shown in Figure 13-1 — in case they're too ambitious for your lifestyle or you can bump them up for an added challenge. The companion Activity app for iPhone shows you additional information, including a historical look at your Activity levels. Plus, every Monday, you should receive a summary report on your Apple Watch about your activity and goals.

Chapter 8 offers a closer look at the Activity and Workout apps.

Did you know you could multitask on Apple Watch? It's true. While you're not seeing two apps on the screen at the same time, you can quickly double-tap the Digital Crown button to switch to your last used app. For example, you can toggle between the Music app and the Weather app to catch a multiday forecast and then switch back to the Music app again by double-tapping the Digital Crown button — perhaps to change tracks. Because Apple thinks you might want to see the time more than other information, the clock is visible in many apps already; therefore, you don't need to leave the app you're in to see what time it is.

Figure 13-1: You can change your daily goals depending on how ambitious you are.

Apple Pay

Using your watch to buy things at retail is incredibly convenient. Even if you don't have your iPhone around, you can wave your wrist over one of those contactless terminals at the checkout counter or at an Apple Pay–compatible vending machine and the transaction is completed. And securely.

To buy something using Apple Pay on your Apple Watch, follow these steps:

1. **Double-tap the Side button on Apple Watch, which brings up Apple Pay.**

   It uses your default card in the Passbook app, but you can change it to something else if you like. See Chapter 10 for more on the Passbook app.

2. **Hold the watch up to the contactless terminal and you should hear a tone and feel a slight vibration — both of which confirm the payment has been made.**

   That's all there is to it. Apple Pay uses near field communication (NFC) technology inside of Apple Watch to make the *digital handshake* with the retailer's contactless terminal.

Apple Pay is supported by many banks and financial institutions as well as many thousands of retailers. But remember, you need to set up Apple Pay first on your iPhone if you haven't done so already. See Chapter 10 for more on Apple Pay.

Hotel Key

Free apps like Starwood Preferred Guest (SPG) let you tap your watch on your hotel door to gain entrance. No more fumbling for the key card or having it demagnetized because you had it in your pocket with your smartphone.

If you've got the free app installed, tell someone at the check-in desk at a Sheraton, Westin, W Hotel, Meridien, St. Regis, Element, or Aloft. Keep in mind that support for Apple Watch likely won't be available at all Starwood hotels and resorts or rolled out at the same time.

In the near future, expect many similar apps to let you into your car — instead of needing a large key fob — or to enter public transit stations, including bus depots and train terminals. Perhaps soon, Apple Watch will let you walk through your front door at home (with high-tech deadbolts, such as the Kevo from Kwikset) or into your office by tapping your wrist on a card reader.

See Chapter 11 for other third-party Apple Watch apps to check out.

Glances

Swipe up from the bottom of the watch face to access your Glances. These are simple one-screen (nonscrollable) alerts that give you quick information.

Examples of Glances include:

- **Music:** See the current or last-played track, which you can pause, play, or skip forward or backward, and adjust the volume.

- **Heart Rate:** This Glance gives you a look at your heart rate — measured every ten minutes and measured in beats per minute, as shown in Figure 13-2.

✔ **Battery:** See how much power your Apple Watch has remaining, shown by percentage. Tap Power Reserve to extend battery life.

✔ **Activity:** See your daily goals for Move, Exercise, and Stand — illustrated by colored rings — and how well you're doing for each.

✔ **Calendar:** See upcoming events to be aware of. Use Siri to add another one if you like.

✔ **Weather:** See the temperature and weather conditions in your city, including a look at projected highs and lows for the day.

✔ **Stocks:** Check on how an entire exchange is doing or see information on individual public companies you're monitoring.

Figure 13-2: Thanks to the sensors underneath Apple Watch, you can see your heart rate — measured in beats per minute — or even send it to someone who also has an Apple Watch. See Chapter 5 for more on sending your heartbeat to someone.

✔ **Map:** See your location on an overhead map, including nearby streets and local businesses.

✔ **World Clock:** See what time it is in other parts of the world — which you can customize — along with a map of the world with dots to show you where it is.

See Chapter 2 for more on Glances and Notifications.

Apple Watch has Wi-Fi, but that doesn't mean you can surf the web. Wi-Fi is only being used to move or sync data between your Apple Watch and iPhone. That's probably not a bad thing, given the fact Wi-Fi would eat up valuable battery life pretty quickly. Plus, Apple Watch doesn't come with a web browser.

Music Playback

Many people who exercise rely on music to help keep them entertained and motivated. You might not want to bring a large iPhone with you on a jog or run, so Apple thankfully lets you sync some music to Apple Watch — up to 2 gigabytes or about 500 songs.

To sync music to your Apple Watch, follow these steps:

1. **Connect your Apple Watch to your PC or Mac via its USB charger.**

   Use the magnetic charger that shipped with your Apple Watch.

2. **On your iPhone, open the Apple Watch app.**

3. **Under My Watch, scroll down and tap Music, followed by Synced Playlist.**

   Decide what you'd like to transfer over to your watch: My Top Rated, Recently Added, Recently Played, Top 25 Most Played, or Purchased tracks.

4. **Tap to select one of these options.**

   Unplug the Apple Watch from the computer when the sync is complete.

After you have songs stored on your Apple Watch, follow these steps:

1. **Open the Music app and press and hold the screen (Force Touch) to launch a couple options.**

   You should see options for Shuffle, Repeat, AirPlay, and Device.

2. **Tap Device and then select Apple Watch instead of iPhone.**

   You should be prompted to pair a Bluetooth-enabled headset or head-phones to hear the music. The Apple Watch screen shows you what's playing on your watch or iPhone.

Apple Watch also acts as a remote control for an Apple TV connected to a TV, an iTunes library on a Windows PC or Mac, or for playing music on an iPhone or iPad. See Chapter 9 for more on these and other media- and entertainment-related tasks.

Maps

Because Apple Watch is always on your wrist, it's a conveniently placed screen for getting directions. Apple Watch can give you turn-by-turn directions by tapping into your nearby iPhone's GPS chip, and you should see the overhead map on your watch, including a blue dot for your location, a red pushpin for the destination, and the path to take to get there quickly. Apple Watch gently vibrates to tell you when it's time to turn left or right.

To use the Maps app on your Apple Watch, follow these steps:

1. **Press the Digital Crown button to go to the Home screen.**

2. **Tap the Maps app.**

   You can also raise your wrist and say "Hey, Siri, Maps." Either action opens the Maps app. An overhead map of your current location appears on the Apple Watch screen, and you can swipe in any given direction to move the map around or you can twist the Digital Crown button if you want to see nearby streets or businesses.

3. **Press and hold the screen and then speak an address or business name.**

   If you make a mistake, tap Clear. If you're happy with what you requested, continue to the next step.

4. **Tap Start to begin the turn-by-turn directions.**

   You should now see and feel when it's time to turn left or right when nearing an intersection — whether you're on foot or in a vehicle. Your iPhone also shows you information if you want to peek at a bigger screen (safely) or hand it to a passenger. See Chapter 6 for more on the Maps app.

Digital Touch

Many smartwatches on the market offer similar features, such as seeing who's calling or texting, calculating fitness information, or getting directions to a destination.

But Apple Watch offers three unique watch-to-watch communication options — collectively referred to as Digital Touch:

- ✔ **Sketch:** Draw something with your finger and the person you're sending it to sees it animate on his or her Apple Watch.

- ✔ **Tap:** Send gentle (and even customizable) taps to someone to let that person know you're thinking about him or her.

- ✔ **Heartbeat:** Your built-in heart rate monitor is captured and sent to someone special so that person can feel it on his or her wrist.

To send a sketch with your Apple Watch, follow these steps:

1. **Press the Side button, which brings up your Friends ring.**

   You should see up to 12 of your closest friends and family members here.

2. **Twist the Digital Crown button to select someone.**

   After someone is selected, you should see ways to reach out to him or her at the bottom of the screen. If that person has an Apple Watch, you should see an icon of a hand with a forefinger extended.

3. **Tap that icon to send a Digital Touch.**

   Start sketching on the black screen or tap the colored circle at the top of the screen to change colors and then draw something, such as a flower, a heart, a message (as shown in Figure 13-3), and so on.

The person you're sending it to will see the drawing appear on his or her wrist just as you drew it. See Chapters 3 and 5 for more on using Digital Touch.

Figure 13-3: You don't have a lot of screen space to work with, but you can have fun drawing and sending a custom-made design or message to another Apple Watch wearer.

Siri

Because Apple Watch was designed for quick interactions and to get information wherever and whenever you need it most, the best way to interact with your watch is by your voice. Providing you're in a place where you can talk freely, speaking into your watch's microphone is a fast, accurate, and convenient method for getting what you want when you want it.

If you recall, you can use Siri in two ways on Apple Watch:

- **Digital Crown:** Press the Digital Crown button and wait to see the little bars jumping up and down near the bottom of your screen. This confirms Siri is "listening" to you.
- **Voice activation:** Raise your wrist and say "Hey, Siri," followed by your command or question.

For both of these options, you should get what you need within a second or two, but remember, you need your iPhone nearby because your request is quickly sent to Apple's servers to process it.

Siri can help you with virtually any task, including some of the following, which are tied to various apps and online content:

- "What time is it in Milan?"
- "Read me my messages."
- "Text Susan that I'll be five minutes late."
- "Call Dad."
- "Show me my email."
- "When is my next appointment?"
- "Open the Activity app" or "Open the Workout app."
- "Where is the closest gas station?"
- "What song is playing?"
- "Play jazz."
- "What's the weather going to be like tomorrow?"
- "How are the Braves doing?"
- "Set an alarm for 6 a.m."

See Chapter 7 for more on using Siri to help you complete tasks with your Apple Watch.

Watches and Watch Faces

Most companies that release a smartwatch have one model, such as the Moto 360, but Apple Watch is available in two sizes (38 mm and 42 mm), three different materials (aluminum, stainless steel, and 18-karat gold), in multiple case colors, and with various band colors, materials, and styles to choose from.

Clearly, Apple has thought this through.

Even with all the options, the user experience will be similar between all the versions because features, interfaces, and apps are the same for all of them.

The following is a quick summary of the three collections:

- **Apple Sport Watch:** Ideal for those who want something light and durable, Apple Watch Sport is made from anodized aluminum and with sweat-resistant "fluoroelastomer" (synthesized rubber) in five sporty colors: white, black, blue, green, and pink.

- **Apple Watch:** A bump up in price, Apple Watch comes in highly polished stainless steel or matted black stainless steel and with a variety of bands: leather, fluoroelastomer, Milanese loop, and link bracelet.

- **Apple Watch Edition:** Available in rose or yellow 18-karat gold, Apple Watch Edition is more of a luxury timepiece. The retina display is protected by polished sapphire crystal, and the watch offers a number of unique straps and bands, including 18-karat gold clasps, buckles, and pins.

See www.dummies.com/extras/applewatch for more information on the Apple Watch collections and some accessories.

Go for the gold

Some people — nay, many people — thought Apple was crazy to create an 18-karat-gold version of Apple Watch (Apple Watch Edition). Were you one of them? On April 10, 2015, when preorders first went on sale in nine countries, the $20,000 gold Apple Watch Edition model sold out in China in less than an hour.

And once you've got an Apple Watch on your wrist, you've got ten watch faces to choose from — all of which can be personalized to your liking:

- **Astronomy:** An out-of-the-world view of our solar system
- **Chronograph:** Like an analog stopwatch
- **Color:** Classic analog face with customizable colors
- **Mickey Mouse:** A classic returns — and in animation
- **Modular:** Bold digital watch face with lots of options
- **Motion:** Animated objects, such as butterflies and flowers
- **Simple:** A minimalistic but stylish analog watch
- **Solar:** Based on your location and time of day, you can see the sun's position
- **Utility:** Analog watch with optional calendar reminders and more
- **X-Large:** Large digital font for viewing at a distance

See Figure 13-4 for watch face examples, and see Chapter 4 for more on the watch faces and how to customize them.

Figure 13-4: Choose from Astronomy or Mickey Mouse or eight other watch faces to personalize your Apple Watch.

Talk about demand

Even though it was an unproven product for Apple, Apple Watch was a hit right out of the gate. According to Slice Intelligence (`intelligence.slice.com`), an online shopping analytics firm with a panel of more than two million online shoppers in the United States, 62 percent of Apple Watches were sold in the first hour of availability on April 10, 2015; 86 percent sold by 8 a.m. Approximately 1,039,000 people bought 1.4 million Apple Watches. As for which of the three collections sold the most, 62 percent bought Apple Watch Sport (least expensive offering), 38 percent purchased Apple Watch, and less than 1 percent ordered Apple Watch Edition (with an average price of $11,000 apiece).

And speaking of customization, Apple Watch includes ten unique watch faces you can choose from — whether you want a classic analog look, a more modern digital face, or even an animated watch face. Plus, you can customize the color and add complications, which are extra bits of information, such as weather and an alarm clock.

Gaming

It's a huge understatement to say Apple Watch is an unproven video game platform. But given Apple's track record with iOS devices — not to mention a passionate app development community eager to take advantage of this new real estate on the wrist — gaming might be the secret "killer app" of Apple Watch.

You're in line at the supermarket and you want to kill some time by dunking a few virtual baskets by tapping on your watch screen. Or you're on the train to work and you want to use your fingertip to slide letter tiles on a board to create a word. Or perhaps you're walking down the street and you feel a tap on your wrist — an alert that someone is invading your village and you've got to decide what to do.

Just as the smartphone and tablet have become viable gaming platforms in a very short period of time — even pumping out such iconic games as Angry Birds and Flappy Bird — Apple Watch could introduce fresh gaming experiences on a device we always have strapped to our wrists.

Chapter 12 offers a look at a half-dozen games available for Apple Watch, but the App Store — accessible on the companion Apple Watch app on iPhone — has thousands more to choose from. Figure 13-5 shows what Rules! — a popular iOS game — looks like on the Apple Watch (and, yes, it's available for both platforms).

Figure 13-5: A look at Rules! for Apple Watch — based on the popular iOS version.

Index

About the Author

Marc Saltzman is a prolific journalist, author, and TV/radio personality who specializes in consumer electronics, business technology, interactive entertainment, and Internet trends. Marc has authored 16 books since 1996 and currently contributes to more than 40 high-profile publications, including *USA Today*/Gannett, Yahoo, MSN, *AARP: The Magazine*, Common Sense Media, *Costco Connection*, *Metro*, the *Toronto Star*, *Postmedia*, *CAA* magazine, and others. Marc hosts various video segments, including "Gear Guide" (seen at Cineplex movie theaters and sister chains across Canada), and is a regular guest on CNN, CNN International, FOX and CTV's Canada AM. Marc also hosts "Tech Talk," a radio show on Toronto's NewsTalk 1010 and Montreal's CJAD 800 (Bell Media).

Apple Watch For Dummies is Marc's second *Dummies* book. He also penned *Siri For Dummies*.

Follow Marc on Twitter: @marc_saltzman.

Dedication

This book is dedicated to my extraordinary parents, Stan and Honey Saltzman. A heartfelt thank-you for your never-ending support, guidance, and love.

Author's Acknowledgments

I'd like to acknowledge all the talented folks at John Wiley & Sons, for this book wouldn't have happened without their professionalism, patience, and knowledge (hardly *Dummies!*). In particular, I'd like to thank my uber-talented editor Christopher Stolle as well as awesome acquisitions editors Andy Cummings and Steven Hayes.

Publisher's Acknowledgments

Acquisitions Editors: Andy Cummings and Steven Hayes

Project Editor: Christopher Stolle

Copy Editor: Christopher Stolle

Project Manager: Mary Corder

Editorial Assistant: Claire Brock

Sr. Editorial Assistant: Cherie Case

Production Editor: Kinson Raja

Photographer: Marc Saltzman

Cover Image: Marc Saltzman

Apple & Mac

iPad For Dummies,
6th Edition
978-1-118-72306-7

iPhone For Dummies,
7th Edition
978-1-118-69083-3

Macs All-in-One
For Dummies, 4th Edition
978-1-118-82210-4

OS X Mavericks
For Dummies
978-1-118-69188-5

Blogging & Social Media

Facebook For Dummies,
5th Edition
978-1-118-63312-0

Social Media Engagement
For Dummies
978-1-118-53019-1

WordPress For Dummies,
6th Edition
978-1-118-79161-5

Business

Stock Investing
For Dummies, 4th Edition
978-1-118-37678-2

Investing For Dummies,
6th Edition
978-0-470-90545-6

Personal Finance
For Dummies, 7th Edition
978-1-118-11785-9

QuickBooks 2014
For Dummies
978-1-118-72005-9

Small Business Marketing
Kit For Dummies,
3rd Edition
978-1-118-31183-7

Careers

Job Interviews
For Dummies, 4th Edition
978-1-118-11290-8

Job Searching with Social
Media For Dummies,
2nd Edition
978-1-118-67856-5

Personal Branding
For Dummies
978-1-118-11792-7

Resumes For Dummies,
6th Edition
978-0-470-87361-8

Starting an Etsy Business
For Dummies, 2nd Edition
978-1-118-59024-9

Diet & Nutrition

Belly Fat Diet For Dummies
978-1-118-34585-6

Mediterranean Diet
For Dummies
978-1-118-71525-3

Nutrition For Dummies,
5th Edition
978-0-470-93231-5

Digital Photography

Digital SLR Photography
All-in-One For Dummies,
2nd Edition
978-1-118-59082-9

Digital SLR Video &
Filmmaking For Dummies
978-1-118-36598-4

Photoshop Elements 12
For Dummies
978-1-118-72714-0

Gardening

Herb Gardening
For Dummies, 2nd Edition
978-0-470-61778-6

Gardening with Free-Range
Chickens For Dummies
978-1-118-54754-0

Health

Boosting Your Immunity
For Dummies
978-1-118-40200-9

Diabetes For Dummies,
4th Edition
978-1-118-29447-5

Living Paleo For Dummies
978-1-118-29405-5

Big Data

Big Data For Dummies
978-1-118-50422-2

Data Visualization
For Dummies
978-1-118-50289-1

Hadoop For Dummies
978-1-118-60755-8

Language &
Foreign Language

500 Spanish Verbs
For Dummies
978-1-118-02382-2

English Grammar
For Dummies, 2nd Edition
978-0-470-54664-2

French All-in-One
For Dummies
978-1-118-22815-9

German Essentials
For Dummies
978-1-118-18422-6

Italian For Dummies,
2nd Edition
978-1-118-00465-4

 **Available in print and e-book formats.**

Available wherever books are sold. **For more information or to order direct visit www.dummies.com**

Math & Science

Algebra I For Dummies,
2nd Edition
978-0-470-55964-2

Anatomy and Physiology
For Dummies, 2nd Edition
978-0-470-92326-9

Astronomy For Dummies,
3rd Edition
978-1-118-37697-3

Biology For Dummies,
2nd Edition
978-0-470-59875-7

Chemistry For Dummies,
2nd Edition
978-1-118-00730-3

1001 Algebra II Practice
Problems For Dummies
978-1-118-44662-1

Microsoft Office

Excel 2013 For Dummies
978-1-118-51012-4

Office 2013 All-in-One
For Dummies
978-1-118-51636-2

PowerPoint 2013
For Dummies
978-1-118-50253-2

Word 2013 For Dummies
978-1-118-49123-2

Music

Blues Harmonica
For Dummies
978-1-118-25269-7

Guitar For Dummies,
3rd Edition
978-1-118-11554-1

iPod & iTunes
For Dummies, 10th Edition
978-1-118-50864-0

Programming

Beginning Programming
with C For Dummies
978-1-118-73763-7

Excel VBA Programming
For Dummies, 3rd Edition
978-1-118-49037-2

Java For Dummies,
6th Edition
978-1-118-40780-6

Religion & Inspiration

The Bible For Dummies
978-0-7645-5296-0

Buddhism For Dummies,
2nd Edition
978-1-118-02379-2

Catholicism For Dummies,
2nd Edition
978-1-118-07778-8

Self-Help & Relationships

Beating Sugar Addiction
For Dummies
978-1-118-54645-1

Meditation For Dummies,
3rd Edition
978-1-118-29144-3

Seniors

Laptops For Seniors
For Dummies, 3rd Edition
978-1-118-71105-7

Computers For Seniors
For Dummies, 3rd Edition
978-1-118-11553-4

iPad For Seniors
For Dummies, 6th Edition
978-1-118-72826-0

Social Security
For Dummies
978-1-118-20573-0

Smartphones & Tablets

Android Phones
For Dummies, 2nd Edition
978-1-118-72030-1

Nexus Tablets
For Dummies
978-1-118-77243-0

Samsung Galaxy S 4
For Dummies
978-1-118-64222-1

Samsung Galaxy Tabs
For Dummies
978-1-118-77294-2

Test Prep

ACT For Dummies,
5th Edition
978-1-118-01259-8

ASVAB For Dummies,
3rd Edition
978-0-470-63760-9

GRE For Dummies,
7th Edition
978-0-470-88921-3

Officer Candidate Tests
For Dummies
978-0-470-59876-4

Physician's Assistant Exam
For Dummies
978-1-118-11556-5

Series 7 Exam For Dummies
978-0-470-09932-2

Windows 8

Windows 8.1 All-in-One
For Dummies
978-1-118-82087-2

Windows 8.1 For Dummies
978-1-118-82121-3

Windows 8.1 For Dummies,
Book + DVD Bundle
978-1-118-82107-7

 **Available in print and e-book formats.**

Available wherever books are sold. **For more information or to order direct visit www.dummies.com**

Take Dummies with you everywhere you go!

Whether you are excited about e-books, want more from the web, must have your mobile apps, or are swept up in social media, Dummies makes everything easier.

Leverage the Power

For Dummies is the global leader in the reference category and one of the most trusted and highly regarded brands in the world. No longer just focused on books, customers now have access to the For Dummies content they need in the format they want. Let us help you develop a solution that will fit your brand and help you connect with your customers.

Advertising & Sponsorships

Connect with an engaged audience on a powerful multimedia site, and position your message alongside expert how-to content.

Targeted ads • Video • Email marketing • Microsites • Sweepstakes sponsorship

Dummies products make life easier!

- DIY
- Consumer Electronics
- Crafts
- Software
- Cookware
- Hobbies
- Videos
- Music
- Games
- and More!

For more information, go to **Dummies.com** and search the store by category.

FOR
DUMMIES
A Wiley Brand